To Touch a Butterfly

Rachel Farrington-Allen

Note for Librarians: A cataloguing record for this book is available from Library and Archives Canada at www.collectionscanada.ca/amicus/index-e.html
ISBN 1-4120-5514-8

Printed in Victoria, BC, Canada. Printed on paper with minimum 30% recycled fibre. Trafford's print shop runs on "green energy" from solar, wind and other environmentally-friendly power sources.

TRAFFORD
PUBLISHING™

Offices in Canada, USA, Ireland and UK
This book was published *on-demand* in cooperation with Trafford Publishing. On-demand publishing is a unique process and service of making a book available for retail sale to the public taking advantage of on-demand manufacturing and Internet marketing. On-demand publishing includes promotions, retail sales, manufacturing, order fulfilment, accounting and collecting royalties on behalf of the author.

Book sales for North America and international:
Trafford Publishing, 6E–2333 Government St.,
Victoria, BC v8t 4p4 CANADA
phone 250 383 6864 (toll-free 1 888 232 4444)
fax 250 383 6804; email to orders@trafford.com
Book sales in Europe:
Trafford Publishing (uk) Limited, 9 Park End Street, 2nd Floor
Oxford, UK oxi 1hh UNITED KINGDOM
phone 44 (0)1865 722 113 (local rate 0845 230 9601)
facsimile 44 (0)1865 722 868; info.uk@trafford.com
Order online at:
trafford.com/05-0412

10 9 8 7 6 5 4

Contents

Acknowledgements

I originally started this book for myself and for my daughter, Lucie, although she is too young to yet read it, to tell her what has made her Mum into the person she is today, however, it became so much more to me. There have been many people who have helped me along the way, by offering their counsel, friendship or opinion. So here goes with my thanks and if I forget anyone, I do apologise, you know who you are if you have helped and I will thank each and every one of you personally!

A special thank you to my best friend, Lara Oakes, not only for your support in this book, but also over the last 11 years. You've listened to me, cried with me and supported me through everything. I love you honey and I'm glad the blanks are finally filled in for you!

To my parents and my sister for being the flip side to this coin during my childhood and giving me the stability back then I wouldn't have survived without. H, there will always be clowns to the left of us.....

Special thanks to Tony McEwan, Julie O'Rourke, Benjamin Hartley, Janet Goodwin, Lynsey Price, Kirsty Banim, Julia Horner, Martin Illidge, Martin Bailey, David Hesketh and of course my best friend Daniel Read. To Neil Farrington for giving me the most beautiful children a Mum could wish for. To Irvin Allen, the courageous girls who attended the NSPCC course with me, Mr Grimes, Mrs Howard-Haggerty, Mrs Barratt (for being truly inspirational teachers), Sally Keck and to my Aunty Julie for standing up for me when no one else would. To Bill Beswick for your friendship and counsel. To Emmanouil Vrentos for giving me a happy ending to my butterfly tale, Mark Southall, the Donlan's; Alice, John and Kate for taking me in when I was at my lowest ebb and being an extended family to me.

A huge thank you goes to Sarah Newcombe of Trafford Publishing for putting up with the flakiest and most evasive writer in history. I owe you a debt of gratitude for your patience and perseverance.

Thank you to my gorgeous princess, Lucie. Honey you are the best thing I ever did and I love you the whole world and the moon and the stars and Jupiter and Mars.

Out of respect and privacy some of the names in this book have been changed.

This book is dedicated to Lucie and the memory of Jamie.

Forethought

I would have liked to have started my story with 'Once Upon a Time...' as I did as a child, however, I am led to believe that to start a story like this is something they ask children not to do as it insinuates a fairytale. Although I am no longer a child obviously and this is not a fairytale by any stretch of the imagination, it's my tale. Besides, I've never been one to conform though so here goes.

Once upon a time there lived a family – a middle class, hard working, family - two loving, caring parents, with two children, girls, my sister Grace and I. We lived in a nice area, in a large house, with a beautiful oak tree in the back garden. We were the perfect, idyllic family from the out-side. Inside however, I harboured a secret that has spoilt this squeaky clean image, tarnished it, taken it away, made it unclean. This is my story, the story of my secret, the skeleton in my closet. It is written for me, about me, to exorcise my demon.

Once upon a time before I was robbed of my innocence...

Chapter 1

My Family

To define whether my family is a normal family you have to look at the definition of family within society. The Oxford dictionary's definition of a family is an emotionless and cold description. How does society define a good family? Mine are good in my eyes, I have always been happy with them, my parents and my sister. I'm lucky like that - some people have no support, but me, I have everything with them. They love me for who I am and what I have become as an adult. How can one define what is a normal family though? Nowadays in the era of single parent families, this age of political correctness, is there such thing as a normal family? My family is at least close and we love each other with a fierce protectiveness that seems to be becoming more of a rarity these days. Things weren't always so plain sailing for us though. Like any 'family' we have had our differences. We've had problems, mostly caused by me I might add, that I deeply regret now. In my teenage years I was an absolute nightmare, then again what teen-ager do you know that doesn't play up a bit from time to time. I had my reasons.

It's only really now that I have become a parent, that I appreciate the full extent of why my parents worried so deeply about Grace and I. Girls are so bloody difficult. You worry about them constantly – not that I imagine the worry with boys wouldn't be any worse, just different.

To define whether my life has been a good life is the sixty four thousand dollar question for me. I believe my life has been good and I believe that I have learnt from my mistakes and those that have been made around me. I am a stronger person for my experiences and I know I can eventually have the ultimate happiness, by surviving, thriving, making my life the success I deserve, although, to say my experiences haven't changed me as a person would be wrong. They have changed me immensely, deeply and personally which I suppose is why I feel the urge to write them all down, to capture in essence what my happenings have done to me as the person, the mother, the colleague, the lover, the friend.

I know I am a good friend to have, even a good enemy, because I have developed the refusal to say no to anyone and the inability to stay mad. It is built into my chemistry now. Even when it comes to work I can't say no. I can't bear to believe anyone could feel bad about me when actually all I do is run myself ragged, much to the despair of those who are close to me. My life seems to have been about keeping other people happy and when it comes to doing something for me, even if for a self preservation purpose, I don't consider that high priority. Also my inability to deal with hurt. If someone hurts me on an emotional level I bolt so no-one can get through or get in again. I give up then and not only push the person away but anyone who cares, much to the frustration of my family. I believe in my heart that I will be able to block out bad things by pushing everyone. Lastly, I am incredibly malleable in character, easy to manipulate into doing what others want and I rarely stick up for myself. I mean when I lose my temper, I lose it badly and become incredibly stubborn, but I'll do anything to prevent others from feeling angry with me, always testament to my unhappiness. All of these traits I assume are something from my childhood that has scarred me so deeply and will never really change or go away.

As a child, if I saw something broken it would destroy me. I would try to pick it up, fix it, put it all together and then things would be fine. I couldn't even cope with death of small things like ants. I wanted the world to be bright and happy.

I caught a butterfly once, held it in my hands as I rushed home. I was so excited. The butterfly was going to live in my bedroom and be my friend. Mum found me with it and told me that if you touched a butterfly that the dust they had on their wings would come off and they would die. I knew I had touched it and I knew it would die. It was my fault! I'd killed something. I opened my bedroom window but it wouldn't fly away. I'd stolen its spirit. I could still see the dust all over my fingerprints. I was a butterfly murderer! I still think about the feel of the wings, the silky soft flutter in my hand of my new found friend, the excitement of having something which was all mine. We had a cat, Sukey, but she liked Grace more than me. I think I tried too hard to get her to like me by picking her up too much. But this butterfly would be just mine and of course now it was going to die. I dreamt that night that all its butterfly friends would come for me banging against my window dropping all of their dust. I would wake up in the morning and the garden would look like it had snowed, however, this snow wouldn't be white, it would be all the colours of the rainbow and butterfly bodies would litter the garden. I woke up in a sweat. I could still feel the poor thing. Of course it had eventually flown off into the big copse behind the house and I never knew if it survived but I had always hoped it had. I couldn't deal with the concept of pain or hurt let alone death.

I was born into a happy suburban area, my Dad, a successful business man, my Mum at home with us. She worked part time for an Estate Agents at the weekends in the village where we lived. It always smelt of Astral moisturizer whenever we went down there on a Saturday with my Dad. Mum always smelt of it. Even now if you look into her handbag there is that familiar smell emanating from the blue tub.

As I have mentioned before I have an older sister, Grace, with whom I fought all the time until we didn't live together. I never really knew why we fought, I just thought it was sibling rivalry, normal behavior. We are very close now though, closer than we have ever been before.

My first memory is one of the happiest times in my life. I was in Canada, aged two and a half. We stayed with my Aunty Julie in her house, a very typical Canadian house from the pictures I've seen but fairly non-descript in my memory. However, I recall her table – strange I know that I should remember a table and not the house – or maybe it is because I have been told this story so many times, I have conjured it in my head. I remember the shape of it, squ-oval as we call it now. I danced on the table with my new red shoes on and Julie told me if I didn't get down she would smack me. Defiant as only a child can be I said I'd tell my Mum and she laughed, told me to tell her. I didn't. I knew I'd have got what we called 'done', for dancing on the table. I wouldn't have done it at home but Julie always brought out the rebel in me. I had always loved the thrill of new shoes, even now I'm obsessed with them. I have pairs in every conceivable colour. The difference is now that I normally only wear them once and then they live in a box to stop them from getting dusty – back then shoes were practical. Mum and Dad were comfortable in their earnings but we never had more than one pair of shoes at a time, I suppose this is because they were so expensive. I loved going into Clarks in the village and putting my feet into the measuring machine that moved in from the sides as if to crush your feet but stopped just in time to give you a perfect guide of your size and width. The rows upon rows of little green boxes I could see through the curtain in the back of the shop fascinated me and in my dreams I'd own all of them, getting my professional shoe-fitter to measure my feet each day to decide which ones I'd wear. I once saw the most gorgeous pair of patent shoes in the window, they were black, so shiny you could see your face in them. I begged Mum to take me back to the shops in the village so I could show her these shoes and subsequently cried my heart out when I wasn't allowed to have them because they were 'slip-ons' and therefore 'too grown up'. Grace had slip-ons, a purply pink pair with a little tassle on the front and tartan on the inside lining. She had begged for them and Mum had caved. They fell off her feet so much in the end Mum had to buy a pair of insoles to go inside. They were so cool. It wasn't fair, she got everything!

During our time in Canada we drove one day up into the mountains to a place called Lake Minnewonka. Grace and I had our photograph taken together in the grass. The lake was cold although it was a beautiful sunny day. Mum and Dad were close and it was during a time when Grace was still quite protective of me, the bickering only grew the older I got. My life seemed perfect. We paddled in the lake as a family. It was freezing, fed by the glacier and we waved furiously at a speedboat as it went past us, everyone else laughing as the waves lapped up to their knees. But of course I was only two and the waves washed the full height of my body. The cold brought panic to me as it took my breath away. I've never forgotten that panic. That feeling of being encompassed by a power I had no control over. I've hated the cold ever since that day.

There was the most frightening drop in the lake. It went out for a few feet where the water was so crystal clear it looked like you could have just dipped a glass in and drunk it. The pattern of the sunshine was swirling on top of the water and reflecting onto the pebbles below. Then a few feet away the drop, so sheer and intense into the black depths of the water, so steep my eyes were like saucers as I could only imagine where it would lead to. Probably hell! This was back when I believed in such things as heaven and hell. Back when I believed that there was a good power that would protect all innocent human beings, although I couldn't have vocalised that.

,,

That's all I remember of Canada which is sad because it would probably have been the best holiday ever. The year was 1978, my family were all there, I was safe, secure and loved.

Dad hasn't always been the most demonstrative of people but I've always known he loves me. He'd always been scared of hurting Grace and me because he was so heavy handed and huge. Dad was my hero as a child. He was bigger than all the other Dads and he was respected. Everybody loved him. He was this great big hulk of a man, who despite having no cape and not wearing his underpants on the outside, had super human powers as far as I was concerned. Dad had this ability to make me feel on top of the world. He was my security blanket, my best friend, my comforter, my first aider, my special and wonderful Dad. He made everything that we did a bit magical, everything he touched came to life and his stories, well, they were superb. He had the most infectious laugh, still does. I love it when he laughs as it comes from his belly.

He was usually busy during the week as most fathers were. He came home late each night from a hard day's work in the bank to my Mum who always had tea on the table waiting for him. We would normally be bathed and ready for bed, if it was bath night (Sunday night whether we needed it or not!), two gleaming kids, homework done, teeth brushed and 'shiny halo' hair. The perfect family. Every night Dad used to tuck me in at bedtime. It wasn't that I didn't love Mum, because I did obviously, she's my Mum, but nothing made me feel more secure than having my Dad sit on the bed. He used to put his arms to either side of me, on top of the duvet and lean over whilst we chatted. Sometimes he would tell me something that had happened during the day or he would tell me a story. One of my favourites was about his cat Whiskers. He'd had Whiskers when he was a little boy. Whenever he talked about this I got a picture in my head of this dirty school boy, with mucky knees and a cheeky grin, a bit like Just William. I loved to think of Dad like that, being a cheeky boy, I suppose it's because I was a bit cheeky too. I had the same face as Dad as a boy but obviously longer hair. Grace had the face of an angel so she could get away with anything but my face was always guilty. My Aunty Jill once told me I have the most expressive eyes she's ever seen. She said you could tell how I was feeling by looking into my eyes. Anyway, Dad would sit on the bed putting his arms either side and talk to me and I would feel like I was the most secure, loved person in the whole world. He'd stroke my hair and say 'She's loved' in his soft, well spoken voice. He was always gentle.

When Grace and I had to learn our times tables Dad made flash cards with the sums on the front and the answers on the back. To this day if Dad asks us any of our times tables we can recite them with great ease. He always spent every Sunday with us, without fail. We walked somewhere or played cricket or went to a park, went swimming, or on a trip, saw friends, we always had something to do. He kept us occupied from such an early age and, although Grace seemed to be slightly closer to Mum, I was his shadow. I was always draped around him in some, way shape or form. Even up to being a teenager at night when we watched the television I had some part of me touching Dad. He was always so toasty and warm and he smelt familiar. The warmest thing about my Dad though is his heart. He is a kind and fair man, a gentle giant who would help anyone before himself. One of his former managers had told him that he thought Dad's problem was that if he was in a shipwreck he would be trying to sound the alarm, loading women and children into the boats, steering the ship away from danger, shooting at sharks, finding and firing the panic flares, unhooking lifeboats and handing out life jackets. His boss said that what he should have been doing is standing on peoples heads to get himself to safety where he could then get help to all of these people, he said that of the two, the latter would save more people. However, that was and is my Dad, too kind for his own good. God knows I've put him through enough and yet he still gives me any bit of help, advice or support that I need. I must infuriate the hell out of him but that's daughters for you!

I can't ever remember hearing my Dad swear until I was in my late teens. My and Grace's husbands assure me that his language is very choice on the golf course. But to me my Dad will always be the perfect gentleman.

He was brought up in Hulme, central Manchester, by a well respected family in the neighbourhood. He was named after his Uncle Leo, a force to be reckoned with when Dad was growing up by all intents and purposes. Leo and his brothers were hard as nails and if you upset one you upset the lot. Leo's sister Edith was my Grandma Smith, my dad's mum. I never met her. She died shortly after Dad met Mum. Dad's father was another gentleman in all senses of the word. Mum says that Granddad Smith would have given you the shirt off his back if he thought you wanted it. She said when she used to go round after work after Edie had died, he'd say to her 'Do you want a cuppa tea lovey?' She'd obviously say yes and he'd reply 'Here are pet, you can have mine' and push his cup of tea over the table for her to drink straight away. Granddad Smith had done his National Service in Egypt and subsequently had been away for a lot of my Dad's siblings lives. During this time Dad had been cared for by Edie, Uncle Leo and his older sister Sandra. Edie worked three jobs to support her family and they all lived together along with Dad and his elder brother, Arthur in a small homely flat. In the pictures they look like any ordinary family of the time, the difference being that they were as close knit as anything.

When Granddad Smith got back from his service he ploughed all his energies and efforts into being with my Dad, giving him a love of the cinema, football and cricket. Dad has many of stories about Old Trafford as a boy when his Dad had rushed to get him a ticket or the money for the entrance fee so that his pride and joy could go and watch his team. All Dad's family are devoted Manchester United fans. In fact we worked it out that his Uncle Leo has been going to games at Old Trafford for 80 years now. That's some record really. I don't think there are many who can say the same. Subsequently because his Uncle Leo had always been there for my Dad, he was fiercely protective of his name sake.

There was one particular incident when one of the players, Ronnie Cope, had been angered by a decision by the referee and he booted the ball into the crowd in frustration and it hit my Dad full on in the face, knocking him over! He says he remembers looking up in a daze as the crowds parted for Uncle Leo to walk through. Leo had to be restrained by the stewards because he wanted to go onto the pitch and sort out Ronnie!

Dad was surrounded by strong male role models, all men who could be looked up to and all of whom were very proud that "their little Leo", which still amuses me to this day as Dad is six foot three, had made it into the bank, got his banking exams and was the first one to have a colour television in the family.

It hit Dad very hard when he lost his father. Mum's Dad kind of took over and they became good friends.

Mum was different to Dad again. Everything about Mum was soft and kind, as with Dad, but she had the compassion, the emotional side, the ability to be able to tell me she loved me a billion times a day without it ever losing any of its shine. She and I had a special code for telling each other we loved the other. She would squeeze my hand three times which meant 'I love you'. I would do it back three times which meant 'I love you'. She would do it three times again for 'bet you don't' and I did it back for 'bet I do'. It was special to us and it meant we could say it anytime we needed reassurance without feeling daft.

Whilst Dad provided for us and was all the things a Dad he should be – tough, strong, silent and giving; Mum was the softness. She had this unbelievable knack of being able to tap into how I was feeling. If I felt sad and I saw Mum I could curl myself into her warm stomach and she would cup her hand around my head and make me feel ok, or make me cry, depending on which was required. Mum always used to come in and sit with me after I'd had a nightmare. She used to talk about being in a field, or a meadow, or planning a holiday and all the things we would need to take with us. She would stroke my temples and my hair as she verbally packed our cases, talked me through the journey, took me to this shiny happy place, after, of course, she had turned over the pillow and thrown the bad dream away.

She could get rid of dreams with such ease, she had that magic about her. She made everything fun. Baking, cooking, working, cleaning, everything. She had a song to go with every job and of all the Mum's in the playground she was the most beautiful. She was always smiling, always laughing, joking but most of all she was always mine. Grace and I had a few problems at school, Grace more in her primary years than me, and Mum was always the first one to stand up and fight for us even if we were in the wrong she would defend our actions to the hilt. She was as every Mum should be the person who when all else fails could make us smile without actually doing anything.

As with Dad, Mum and I fought through my teenage years, however, she always listened to me and we were close even though we clashed frquently I always told her what I was getting up to even if it was bad. There are very few things Mum doesn't know about me. She knows the real Rachel, not the painted face that most get, and even if sometimes she doesn't like what she sees she can always see my reasoning and logic and we are always friends. I count her amongst my few best friends, people I couldn't live without. I know one day she won't be there and I will have to deal with my life without her. That day will be the day I will feel her stroking my temples in my sleep, just as I felt the butterfly's wings in my hands well after it had flown away. Her magic dust could never wear off. It is in my blood. I can't imagine my life without her. She visits her sisters in Canada each year for a few weeks and I hate it when she's away for so long because I miss her so desperately. One of my ex boyfriends used to joke that we need to be in walky talky contact!

When she lost her Mum, my Nana, Rosie, it nearly destroyed her and although they were close they weren't nearly as close as we were. However, Mum just seems to bounce back from whatever life can throw at her. She's always been emotional which is where I have inherited the ability to cry at the drop of a hat from. I can cry so easily now that I sometimes wonder whether the tears are for real of whether I have drunk too much during the day and its overflowing. I've been on anti-depressants for as long as I can remember and should be numb to the tears but thank god each day that I can cry because if I couldn't I wouldn't be able to cope with my life.

I will always be proud of Mum and what she had achieved out of her life. She was brought up in a suburb of Manchester, back when it was a gorgeous place to live, back when if you were from there you were fairly well to do. It's now one of the only places on the planet where the bars are on the inside of the pub windows as well as the outside, to prevent people from being thrown out! They have invested a lot of money into it recently and it has improved slightly but not much.

Mum had a few jobs after she left school as she was one of very few of her era that did A Levels. There was no money for Higher Education so she moved into clerical work, as all intelligent girls did, working at the Town Hall. She also worked in various jobs to bring in extra money when she and Dad were planning to get married. The first home they ever had together was a flat above one of the offices of the company Dad worked for. They had to come home from work and start cleaning the bank to subsidise the rent so they could afford it. Dad always tells me a story of the first Christmas they were together and he couldn't afford a tree on his salary. On the last day before he broke up for Christmas he was given a bonus from work. He rushed out and bought a Christmas tree and some small lights and hung them around the window. He bought a fairy to go on top. When Mum got home she was so chuffed she cried. I remember thinking this was the most touching, romantic story I had ever heard. It was a real life fairytale with my parents as the prince and princess. I didn't see the tragedy behind it that so many young couples had to struggle to keep their heads above water as you don't see things like that as a child, you just see the romance.

Mum subsequently studied for and obtained her degree in English at Manchester University when I was five, and then went on to do her teacher training in the Isle of Man. She became an excellent, well respected and liked teacher known for her dedication, obtaining a letter of recognition from the Minister for Education at the time, Estelle Morris, on her retirement.

Anyway, when Mum was younger her family were fairly middle class for her era. Her Dad worked at a local electronics factory after coming out of national service where he flew the Lancaster. Her Mum, Rosie, was such a sweet lady. Everybody liked "that kind Mrs Mainwaring". She was the type of lady who always had sweets in her bag and smelt of talc. She didn't have a bad word to say about anyone. After my Granddad died, she used to come over every Sunday without fail and have lunch with us. You could say to her sit in the chair, read the paper and don't breathe, and she'd sit in the chair, read the paper and she wouldn't breathe! She was about five foot tall which is strange because Mum is five foot nine. Before she became ill at the end of her life she was, as every Nan should be, cuddly. She had the most enormous chest I have every seen and every day she used to pin her bra and her knickers together underneath her clothes with the type of nappy pins we used to have on our terry nappies when we were babies. Those pins must have been older than her.

Nana, was where Mum gets her soft touch from. Mum is one of four girls, Mary, Jill, Julie and Mum. Mary was the first born of Nana and Granddad however she died aged four of a brain tumour. Nana said Granddad was away on National Service at the time and he had time off to come home to spend some time with his wife. Nana never really recovered from Mary's death. We all expect to bury our parents but no parent should have to bury a child. Jill was the next born. Jill was a very sickly child and spent a lot of her time either in bed or in hospital, subsequently, Julie who was next born felt very pushed out, through no fault of her own or Jill's. Not for want of trying on Nana's part, she always treated the girls equally and always used to say that Julie came along at just the right time as she had desperately longed for a healthy child, exactly as Julie was. Julie had real spirit as a child, cheeky and mischievous. Then came my Mum.

Mum was born with thick blonde curly hair, she was a beautiful happy child. She always had ringlets in because Nana used to love putting rags in the girls hair. Mum was always smiling in photographs we have. She seemed to be the perfect child. She had always been frightened of her Dad as he was a very cruel father. He drank a lot. He had a vile temper. It amazes me how Nana and Granddad got together because they were so different.

Mum dated a few people before she met Dad but nobody serious. In fact I think she originally dumped one of Dad's friends to go out with him and I could see why, Dad was really handsome. She had her heart broken by a man called Ken, which always used to make me giggle as a child, because of course your Mum can't have lived before you, yet alone cried over a man!

She was in a local Manchester pop group as a backing singer with her best friend Denise. She was a seemingly quite good child although had her moments of being wild as we all do. Her upbringing, the softness of Nana combined with the harshness of my Granddad, has made her a fantastic parent, as she had both ends of the extreme. She never asked me what it was I had drawn as a child, only asked me to tell her about it. She made every picture feel special, each piece of writing seem like the most important thing she had ever read and every thought or dream seem within my reach. She created a stable family home for us all. She was consistent, caring and loving, as every good Mum should be.

Grace had always been clingy towards Mum. Being born three years before me she had had three years of being completely spoilt with affection and love by Mum and Dad and then along I came to shatter the peace. Mum said that the day she went into hospital and Nana came to look after Grace, she stood on the stairs, kicked Nana with all her might and shouted 'I want my Mummy!'. However, they handled my birth very well. I 'bought' her a present, and on my first return from the hospital, it was wrapped up in the blanket with me. She thought I was so clever from then on. She used to stop people in the street and say 'This is my new sister'. She was devoted. There are numerous photographs of her bathing me dressed as a nurse, cuddling me protectively, staring at me adoringly, of course that didn't last once I got old enough to want to play with her, and subsequently her toys.

Grace had the bigger bedroom at home. Hers had been extended across half of the front of the house in Bramhall which was where I was born. I remember her room had the spookiest posters in of Abba. She used to try to scare me be telling me that they were alive because wherever you moved in the room their eyes followed you. I don't think I slept for a week and it certainly put me off sneaking into her room to play with the 'big girl' toys. A child of her times Grace loved all things Abba and Bucks Fizz. She was always quite meticulous about her bedroom and her toys so when I tipped up putting my mucky fingers on her stuff needless to say it went down like a bucket of cold sick!

And so started our hate-hate relationship. Probably based on the fact that we were so alike, apart from in tidiness, and the fact that we loved each other so much. We fought from that point until the day she moved out to live with her boyfriend in her first flat, which was one of the worst days of my life because I lost my sister's company at home. However, we became best friends. Once we didn't live together the stuff we shared didn't matter. Being the same dress size, shoe size and bra size we had always clashed. Now it became a vast shared wardrobe spread between two homes. Life at home was never really the same after she'd gone and even though she only lived a few miles down the road, it felt so quiet without her, I'd have given anything to have her back. I wanted so much to be like her. She was so beautiful, worldly, pure and so much fun. She had a wicked sense of humour which as we became friends we realised we shared. I will always be sorry for the amount we fought because it was probably more my fault than hers. I smoked, she hated it. I borrowed her stuff, she hated it. I had no money, she had loads. I was a slacker, she was a worker. I used her make-up which was really expensive, mine was the cheap stuff from the chemist in the village, she hated it. We sat down a few years ago and apologised to each other for all the times we called each other names when we were younger.

We very rarely argue now. I know she understands me most of the time although there are times when she is as perplexed by me as she would be by quantum physics.

She lives just round the corner from me now. She got married to Benjamin five years ago which is where I met my husband. I'd just come out of yet another failed relationship. One of many with a succession of older married men after my first marriage ended miserably. She has a little girl now, who is a little ray of sunshine. I look after her three days a week whilst she works. She enjoys being with me although I think at the weekend when she sees me she doesn't like me because she thinks that either Mum, Dad or both are about to disappear because here comes Aunty Rach.

My daughter, gets on famously with the baby. However, Lucie would get on famously with anybody. She is a beautiful girl. Everyday I am in awe of what she achieves and accomplishes and she is by far the best thing I have ever done in my life. She is my reason for being, the reason I am still here today, the only thing that can pull me through my darkest or most desperate times and with little or no effort of her part. All she has to do is smile and I feel alive.

Chapter 2

And it Begins

Every family although seemingly perfect on the outside is riddled with secrets and skeletons, mine being no exception. For as long as I can remember I've been an insecure girl almost as though things weren't quite right inside although I couldn't quite put my finger on why. I didn't know it was wrong. Why would I know? I only knew it felt wrong.

My happy 'before' life changed in the spring of March 1981, on or around my fifth birthday. As a child I don't recall many dates, it's not something I was conscious of but in my head it is always my birthday. It was a really sunny day. Something that I have noticed over the years is that my birthdays are very rarely a nondescript day weather wise. For several years in a row sunshine, for three years we had inches of snow, then years of sunshine again, but never just rain, never dull.

The old oak tree outside Nana's house was moving in the breeze and it was casting shadows across the houses across the way. Nana's house was a very typical Mancunian house of its time. Across the way from it there was a triangular grass verge with road all around and the houses on the other side were beyond that. There weren't many cars ever parked on the street because the area was quite poor. The tree in the front was enormous. It seemed to reach to heaven, higher than mountains, and it was surrounded by Hydrangea bushes. The sickly sweet smell of the purple and blue flowers always lingered up the path and just beyond the double gates at the front. Each of the patio slabs at the front of the house seemed to have a story to tell, covered in moss and footprints of my Mum's childhood. The house always smelt the same, the living room of the gas fire, talc and Murray Mints, Nana's favourite sweets. The kitchen always smelt of a mixture of Granddad's fermenting wine and talc. The kitchen was one of the only warm rooms in the house. Whenever you stayed at Nana's and got into bed the covers were heavy with that cold, damp feel, as she packed you underneath what felt like twenty heavy blankets you could feel the cool slowly creeping through from the bottom of the bed, taking over your body sending you into a heavy sleep. I used to love making those beds with her when we went over because there were so many sheets to tuck in and it seemed far more exciting than our boring old duvets at home to have all those blankets. Again sheets were far more romantic to a little girl of five.

We slept in the back room upstairs together when we stayed and we had a potty in the room because they were scared of us going downstairs at night and falling. I hated having to use that potty, because I was a big girl now. It didn't feel clean. They left the light on in the room so we didn't get scared. It had one of those really dull bulbs in that didn't give off much light at all but just gave enough for us to be able to make out shapes. We were always kept up by the noise of planes taking off and landing at Manchester Airport. I used to lie in that bed at night, there were two in the room, the one nearer the window was mine, and dream I was on a plane, on the journey Mum used to talk about when I'd had a nightmare. It took my mind off making shapes out of clothes in the room. I could always make animals. One night I was so convinced that one of Nana's dressing gowns was a lion that I screamed out and Granddad came running in. He got into bed with me and put his arms around me pulling me close to his chest. His pyjamas were open at the top and I could see a few of the hairs on his brown chest poking through from where the buttons should be. He smelt of Whisky, soap and aftershave and he stayed with me until I fell asleep again. In the morning he said I shouldn't tell anyone he had got into bed with me because 'they might get the wrong idea'. I didn't understand what he meant but I didn't care, he had made the lion go away and that's all I was bothered about.

As I sat watching the shadows the tree was creating across the road and the neighbouring houses from the front room I could hear Nana getting ready to go out. I wanted to stay here forever today. It felt familiar to me. I wanted to play with the brass statues Nana kept on the fire place, the bear, the piano, the spinning wheel. I wanted to clean Nana's spoons with the Brasso that smelt so good. I wanted to make them sparkle and shine better than they ever had before because that's what Nana liked. Everywhere she had been in the world Nana had got a teaspoon. We always brought her one back from our holidays, as did all her friends. She had hundreds on little wooden display racks, most of them shaped like the Maple leaf of the Canadian flag, which is where Julie and Jill had lived for as long as I could remember. I loved rearranging them on those racks. I'd take hours sat at the white kitchen table with the cheap plastic sight seeing mats, scenes of the Rocky Mountains and Canadian lakes, polishing and playing with them. And her fridge magnets, Nana had hundreds of fridge magnets. Grace and I would play swaps with them on the kitchen floor until our legs stuck to the cheap lino. Nana had carpet mats of all different colours, like the ones you get in carpet sample shops, all over the kitchen floor to try to keep it warmer. You always had to be careful when you stepped on them in case they slid. We used to try not to touch the lino on our way from the hall to the back door when we could play outside in the back garden.

I don't know where Grace was this day though. I don't recall her being there. Going to the shops wasn't part of this day. I had plans. But it was ok because Granddad was here and I could stay with him.

I loved my Granddad! I'd heard a lot of stories about him being a drunk and a nasty drunk at that, but to me he was perfect. He did a lot of charity work for the Royal British Legion. When we were young he would take us down to the Legion and buy us a bottle of fizzy pop, usually something exciting like Dandelion and Burdock or Cream Soda, and crisps or nuts and we would be able to talk to his friends. Big Mike his best mate or adopted son as he liked to call himself was my favourite. I never knew why he was called Big Mike or even knew of a Little Mike but he was this huge hulk of a guy and a real sweetheart. He always made me feel like his girlfriend. He made me feel special he used to call me popsy or poppet just like Granddad did. He always bought the best flavour of crisps and never tired of having youngsters around to play with. Mike always had a new joke for me. He was a gentle giant just like my Dad although his language was a bit more choice. 'Salt of the earth' Granddad would say about him. Mike had had some kind of trouble with his family, which is when Granddad had kind of stepped in. Mike's brother Dave was also a good man, looking back on it now they were probably both hard as nails but they were ever so gentle with us.

We used to sit in the function room at the Legion with all the old guys that Granddad must have fought with in the war. They had such interesting stories to tell us about the things they had done and the sights they had seen, although all of them escape me now, I remember I could be transported to a different place altogether as they talked. Because Granddad did a lot of fund raising for the Legion and also helped tremendously when it came to Remembrance Day celebrations, everybody loved him! A fine upstanding member of the community who had fought for his country and returned to help the families of those not quite so fortunate.

So I didn't have to go to the shops with Nana, he was here, albeit a bit drunk but here. I busied myself helping Nana get ready to go. She always took one of those trolleys on wheels with her so that she could pack all her shopping in there and she didn't have to carry bags with her. She used to loop her handbag twice around the handles so no one could steal it, her purse firmly tucked down amongst the hankies, spare rollers, clips, cheap lipsticks, Murray mints and glasses cases she had in there. I never understood why she had so many pair of glasses. I would imagine it was because she was wealthy and glamorous and wanted them to match her outfits. She wrapped her hair into her scarf as she always did, even on sunny days like today, gave me a kiss and set off.

I was alone in the house with him.

All the teaspoons were laid out on the table alongside the Brasso ready for my cleansing touch, but for now I wanted to play with the ornaments on the fireplace. This was the only house I was allowed to play with them and by god was I going to make the most of it. Things like that are important in a child's life. It's the ultimate thrill when you are given something that you can't really play with or you feel that you shouldn't be touching.

In the house we lived in Bramhall, Mum and Dad had had stereo separates. So to record anything onto tape they had to have wires hanging in between each of the unit. They were taping the Sound of Music soundtrack one day and Grace and I had been given strict instructions that we weren't to go in the room because the wires trailed in front of the door. I don't know if I went in because I forgot or whether I was just being mischievous but the next thing was the stereo was in a pile on the floor and Dad was really mad at me. He smacked me, which was something that very rarely happened, and I was sent to my room. It must have been a time my when Aunty Jill was over visiting us from Canada because she came up to see me in my room as I was crying and she couldn't bear for me to cry. The only reason I was crying was because I had a handprint on my leg where Dad had smacked me! I'd always had a thing for touching things which were taboo and the ornaments on the fire were my favourite.

At Nana's the fire was always really warm. It didn't matter what the temperature was like outside, the fire at Nana's house was always lit. My toy ornamental friends and I were in our own world, what with Grace not being there, of course she always got first choice because she was the oldest, but not today. Today they were mine.

Granddad was in the living room with me. He had a glass of whisky in one hand and the back scratcher in the other. The back scratcher was again something Canadian that had been brought back from one of Nana's many trips out there. It was shaped like a totem pole and had animals stuck onto a cream plastic handle, it had words on it but again my memory doesn't serve me well, but I can recall they were red and in capitals.

'Come on', he said 'let me scratch your back'.

'But I'm playing' I said.

'Come on Rach, play with me'.

I could smell the whisky on his breath. He started to touch my shoulder with the scratcher and he was talking quietly. I couldn't hear him very well. His drunken mumblings were always a feature of us being here, that alongside the giggle that he had, almost like the cartoon Scooby Doo. His giggle always made me smile because I would imagine him and Nana as Scooby and Thelma solving the crimes in their spare time. Doing that funny run that cartoons always do when they are trying to get away from the baddies. Nana was like Thelma because she needed her glasses for everything.

I moved over towards him but pulled my toys with me. He often scratched our backs with that scratcher at night when we were watching television with Nana. Particularly after we'd had a bath and were in the living room in front of the fire with our towels on. Nana would have always made us a hot drink. He would only stop scratching to turn the volume down for the adverts or if it was a show where they had lots of cheesy music jingles in like Family Fortunes, which he hated. He always got on his soap box about that. The bear watched him as he crept the scratcher down over the front of my shoulder to my chest. All the time he was touching my hair as he normally did. His talking had stopped and I felt his breath on the back of my neck. He was circling my chest now with the scratcher and he had grip of my hair, not tightly but just so that I felt I couldn't move. It was uncomfortable. I didn't like it.

I could smell the whisky and his Old Spice aftershave. The cat, Whisky, was sitting in the corner of the room sprawled out but his eyes were wide open and he could see I was scared. He stretched his claws out making himself more cosy, but I wasn't cosy, I was ill at ease. My heart was thumping, it felt like it was in my throat. Granddad's hands were moving now, touching my shoulders. He had put the scratcher down and was talking to me.

'Pretty girl' he called me, 'pretty special girl, my special girl'. I said nothing. Looking back now I have always wondered, why did I say nothing? It's a question I've asked myself many times. There were things I knew how to say. I said them to Grace if she picked on me or if she made me feel bad. I could tell her to stop. But he was a grown up I'd get done if I told him to stop. I wanted my Dad, I wanted to hear Nana's keys in the door but she'd only been gone a short while. I knew she wouldn't be back for ages yet. Everybody stops "that nice Mrs Mainwaring" as she walks through the market, for a chat. She knows all the stall owners and they know what she came for. It's her shopping ritual. Besides I know today she will have bought me some cottage cheese and she'll go to the sweet shop on the market. The one where you can get the mix of mints and fruity sweets that she kept in the glass bowl by the side of her chair. She was well liked at all the stalls, as he was at the Legion. She normally went to the post office for some money or the bank and she'd always stop to look in the window of the jewelers. She had a love of anything sparkly. Going into Nana's jewelry box was like going into an Aladdin's Cave. She had two of everything in every colour you could possibly imagine. Beads and stones of blues, reds, yellows, greens all set onto threads or bands of gold. Necklaces, chains, bracelets, watches, brooches, she loved them all, the tackier the better. I wished I was in the Aladdin's Cave now and not here with his hands curling around the front of my chin to my mouth.

He stroked my chin gently and touched the underside of my throat. I had the brass bear in my hand. The bear was also a pencil sharpener as were most of these ornaments we were allowed to play with. The bear was my favourite because it was really cute and if you put it together with the piano it used to look like he was playing it. Bear had his head to one side, he looked happy. I didn't feel happy.

Granddad was stroking one hand up and down on my chest whilst he had firm hold underneath my chin with the other one. I was frozen to the spot. I could feel his hand, warm and almost sticky, holding on tighter, tighter, tighter. I could smell his skin and feel the softness of his palms against me, but he wasn't being gentle or soft today.

'Ever seen a penis' he said. I didn't know what one is, so I shook my head. I had the pencil sharpener in my hand, so perhaps it was a really cool pencil that you can get from Canada and its name is a penis. I waited for him to get up to get it but he didn't. I felt more comfortable now because his hand had moved from my chest. He had moved his hand from my chin down onto my shoulder and the other was in his lap.

'Well, I'll show you my penis if you promise not to tell anyone' he said. The more he talked about the penis the more I wanted to see it. Maybe we could get some paper and draw together with it? Perhaps it was made up of different colours, all my favourites even? He was a very talented artist, really good at drawing and painting. The house was dotted with scenic canvasses he had done from places that they'd been to, photographs they had or postcards from far off lands sent by friends who adored them both. I loved those paintings. He always put his name in the corner like I did at school.

'Turn round, pretty girl' he said. 'Turn round for my penis' and he laughed his giggle, all the time calling me his 'special friend', his 'special girl'. He had his hand in his pants and I see it. Oh no it's where he pees from. That's his penis. I moved to look away but his hand caught my chin and held it in a grip. I didn't want to paint now. I didn't want to colour. The bear was getting hot in my hands and he could still see it too, his faint smile and bright eyes looking at me and the penis. Granddad had my hand in his and he was pulling it towards it. I didn't want to touch it but he made me. At the end it felt soft and dry but in the middle it was wrinkly. His other hand was in my hair now and he was pulling my face towards it. I didn't want it in my face. I found my voice now.

'Can we go to the Legion Granddad?'

'Later, poppet.'

My face was getting closer to his lap. He asked me to suck it like a lolly. I could smell the Whisky now, stronger because he was breathing quite heavily. I could smell his soap, but I couldn't smell any wee.

'Come on take it poppet' he said 'take it'. Just as my mouth was about to touch it he shook and something came out of the end.

'Little virgin girl' he says louder now, almost angry with me. 'Eat it'. I didn't want to. I wanted to cry. It was sticky, like glue and it was on my lips but worst of all it came from where he pees from. But it wasn't wee because it was on my hand and it was white. His penis was smaller now and it was twitching. His breathing had slowed down. 'Go and wash your face poppet,' he said. 'Then we need to talk'.

The cat watched me as I walked to the living room door to go into the bathroom. He finally closed his eyes and fell into his fitful slumber. I still had the bear in one of my hands and his stuff on the other. He hadn't said I should wash my hands so what should I do? I turned on the cold tap and got the face cloth that Nana had left out for me that morning when I'd gone to wash my face and brush my teeth. I wasn't allowed to use the red tap because the water came out fast and got hot really quickly. The taps were always stiff and squeaky at Nana's but her bathroom was older than ours. Ours was a lovely, rich, dark colour not like Nana's which was dull white. The sink was always cold because it was made of an old porcelain that didn't seem to hold any heat at all. The bear looked at me from his perch on the top of the sink as I tried to clean my face, but it still tingled where his wee had been. I buried my face into the cold cloth. It smelt of Nana, talcy, soapy and perfumed. It smelt familiar but far away. It smelt different now, she smelt different, she smelt safe, not of right here, right now but of that morning when I had felt ok. I felt dark now. I had a red dress on with a white stripy bit at the front, it used to one of my favourites but now it felt black. I felt sick. I had to go back into the living room but I didn't want to. I had to go. I decided to wash my hands, but the soap and cold water didn't seem to get them clean or at least they didn't feel clean.

Minutes later when I pushed the door back open to the living room I could hear the television. The fire had been turned up and the room was getting warmer still. The sun was still shining through the back window and outside I could see the sweet peas growing up the wire mesh that Granddad made to help them stand tall. Their window was the kind that had lots of small panes of glass in, separated by wooden, painted frames. There was always a Yucca plant in the window and today I paid particular attention to the little ornamental objects that were there in each individual ledge of each pane of glass, anything to keep my eyes away from the penis. However it was away now. Whilst I'd been in the bathroom it had gone, like it was never there in the first place. Granddad was smiling.

'Fancy going to the Legion poppet' he said, 'your Mum isn't coming for a while yet'.

'Can I clean the spoons?' I said.

'Course you can, but before you do we need to talk. Remember that night when I got in bed with you?' I nodded.

'Well today needs to be like that night, because if your Mummy and Daddy knew then the police would have to come to talk to you and you don't want that do you? You don't want to live in the house for naughty girls do you? I know you're a good girl really but your Mummy and Daddy would be cross and they'd send you away. Wouldn't they?'

I neither nodded nor shook my head, I hadn't known this would happen. How would the police know? I wouldn't tell. No one could see it anymore. I'd washed it off. I wouldn't tell. 'I won't tell I promise' I said looking down at my dress.

Then it struck me, the bear. What if the bear tells Grace? She might tell the police. He had to be my bear. I looked for him but he wasn't in the lounge, he was still in the cold bathroom, not on the fireplace where he belonged all warm and cosy. What about the cat? Would the cat tell? He'd seen it all. He knew how I'd felt, I saw it in his eyes. He was still asleep in the front window waiting for Nana to return with something nice.

'Can I get my bear and clean the spoons?' I asked. 'I promise I won't tell Granddad, cross my heart'. I made the sign of the cross across my heart so that he knew I'd meant it. I didn't want to be sent away. I'd never tell anybody. 'That's my girl' he said 'my special good girl. It's our secret!'. I liked having secrets normally but I didn't like this one. In my life as a parent I have always tried to stress the importance to Lucie of good secrets and bad secrets. Good secrets are something nice like Mummy is getting some flowers as a surprise for Grandma, or the Easter Bunny left an egg for one of her friends. Bad secrets are darker things that make her feel unhappy, alone or uncomfortable. We don't have bad secrets in our house and we don't get

31

cross about anything that someone tells her I will be cross about, even if she has done something wrong.

I collected the bear from the bathroom. He was still sitting on the sink. He didn't look as happy as I whispered my secret into his ear. I took him into the kitchen with me whilst I started to clean the spoons. I hadn't seen my face since he'd put his stuff on there and as I cleaned the spoons I could see how flushed I was in my distorted reflection. I didn't have a mark where he had left his wee, I had got it all off with the cloth, yet where it had been still felt hot and sticky and my lips stung. Would Nana be able to see it? Would she tell the police? I cleaned the spoons as fast as I could making each one gleam and shine. I put then back one by one, for once not rearranging them, sparkling in the wooden racks. She'd know I'd done nothing but cleaned them whilst she was out. She could never know my secret if I'd been busy.

All too quickly I heard her key go in the door and I rushed to greet her enveloping my face in her so she wouldn't see my secret. All my fears were gone as she smiled and brought out the sweets she had got at the market. It was the best sweet shop in the world on the indoor market. It had rows and rows of jars filled with all manner of coloured sugary treats. The shelves seemed to go on forever and the lady that served behind the counter looked like she had a sweet each day from every jar because she was really round and had rosy cheeks. She was a very pretty lady and Nana always stopped to talk to her about what she had been doing in the week.

She took the trolley into the kitchen and unpacked her treats. Cottage cheese for lunch, my favourite. She set about making some "Spam sandwiches" on Blackpool Milk Roll as she always did. Sometimes she bought some spicy sausage from the market as she knew I loved it. Nana was a very typical Nana of her era. She used a lot of tinned products because it was all she was used to. The only fresh things she bought from the market were potatoes, cauliflower and apples. She always had ice cream in the fridge, the type of ice cream that came in a long, thin packet that you could slice a bit off and put it between two wafers. She kept all the wafers and such dry produce in the pantry, a little cupboard with an accordion door next to the fridge in the kitchen. I loved those ice creams she made.

In the kitchen on the wall near the back wall was where all her pots were kept. She had a sliding door cabinet where she kept the tins and things.

Whisky's cat food was in there. One of things I loved doing best was feeding the cat. He was a grumpy old man and you didn't get too close to him because he'd have taken a chunk out of your arm but I still loved the idea that I was giving him something that meant he would live. He loved his milk as well. There was always food just inside the back door, and a saucer of milk for him to drink from.

There was a clock on the wall by the back door, which was ticking loudly. Next to it was a plaque, 'What is a Grandfather?'. The poem that followed was beautiful - sugar coated - but lovely. It has always struck me as strange that they would have that up but old people get bought all kinds of crap and they display it proudly so as not to offend. I always wanted to know who bought it. Maybe I had on one of our holidays? I don't remember.

My bear was on the table looking at me. As long as Nana couldn't see his eyes she couldn't know my secret.

Nana was cheery. She'd seen an old friend at the shops she hadn't seen for ages. 'Next time you'll have to come with me' she said 'instead of busying yourself with all this cleaning. Look at my spoons! They look beautiful'. Next time I would go.

Chapter 3

Sleepless

After I'd blown all of my candles out and all my party guests had gone home, I snuggled in with my Dad on the sofa. My party dress was in the wash covered in cake and all manner of treats and delights and I was in my pyjamas. The teddy I'd had since I was a baby, who traveled everywhere I went was in my hand, the same hand that the stuff had been all over. I smelt his ear. It was my smell. It smelt like home, like safety. He didn't know my secret so he was safe, he was safe for me to be with. I'd had Pinky forever. Whenever Mum washed him in the machine I would get so upset and stand underneath him pegged up on the washing line by his ears sucking his toe. I thought it was so cruel to peg something up by its ears. Grace had always called him Ponky because she said he stank. He didn't stink, he was mine. He smelt clean and fresh, not like me.

Mum tucked me up in bed and I did my usual count to five before I opened my mouth and shouted my Dad to come and tuck me in. Dad sat on the bed putting his arms either side of me. I knew he would be angry if I told him so I didn't. I just carried on as normal. As he walked down the stairs and I looked into the landing light I could feel my tears coming.

'My hands aren't clean, my hands aren't clean!'

I crept into the bathroom and turned on the hot tap. I know I wasn't normally allowed to but I needed to feel ok and I hated the cold. The soap we used at home was always quite hard to get bubbles off and I washed and scrubbed at my hands. Mum shouted up the stairs.

'Rach, are you out of bed?'.

'No' I lied tip-toeing across the landing and hurling myself back into the warmth of my duvet. Tears were now pouring down my face. I couldn't stop thinking about the bear and what he had seen. I could see the sweet peas swimming in front of my eyes. I could hear all the usual sounds from downstairs. Mum was making a cup of tea and the television was on in the living room. We had a pretty living room. It was the colour of warm sunshine. The sofa was dark brown corduroy and the two chairs matched. The television was in the far left hand corner as you walked in the door and it was on the brick and wooden built in unit that ran the length of the wall on that side of the living room that housed the fire and a variety of ornaments and pictures. At the back of the room there was an archway that divided the living room from the dining room. In the dining room there was a beautiful dark oak coloured table and chairs with a matching dresser. The dresser had one of those glass sliding compartments at the top where Mum kept all of her favourite glasses. It had lights built into it that used to make the crystal twinkle as they shone through. Mum and Dad only really used those lights when they had company because it gave off a more flattering glow. They still have that table and chairs now. Mum has wanted a new one for years but Dad can't bear to part with something that has been a part of our family for so many years now. It would be like losing a lifetime of happy memories to get rid of it now. I could almost see them downstairs in my head. They would be watching the news or something equally as boring to a child because of course grown ups didn't watch anything interesting.

Grace had had a friend at my party. So she was tired and was in bed now too.

My silent tears feel thicker, faster. I had to be quiet because if they heard me they'd know. I cried myself to sleep waking up sometime during the night after a nightmare. Mum came in and sat with me whilst I tried to get back off to sleep but for once her soothing didn't work. All I could hear in the journey she was describing was the plane taking off and that just took me to a dark place, a bad place. As soon as she left the room my eyes opened wide. I was waiting for the police to come. I didn't deserve to be here anymore because he had wee'd on me. Mum and Dad would be so angry. They'd think I was naughty, not clean. I'd been so curious about the penis, because I thought we could have painted with it, but I didn't like it and I didn't ever want to see one again.

My friend Sasha had shown me his once, so I knew the difference between boys and girls but his hadn't been big and his wee wasn't white. I know because I'd seen him go to the toilet in the grid at the back of our house many a time when someone else had been on the loo. He didn't want me to put my face near his.

After thinking about this for a while I decided that men shouldn't do that and that I wasn't going to think about it. After all Granddad could forget about it. Why shouldn't I?

As the sun came up I heard the birds start to sing. No planes here to keep me awake I fell into a deep sleep.

It was round about this time that I began to have, what Mum and Dad called, "the screaming abdabs". I used to just scream out in my sleep for no reason. I never woke up. Mum used to come into my room and stroke my head telling me it was just a dream. I used to get fish eyes they said, look really gormless, it became a family joke. Grace had gone through a similar thing crying in her sleep. One night when Mum and Dad had been kept awake for so many nights on the trot Dad had got up, shouted at her and slammed her bedroom door so hard that in the morning he woke up to find all the sealant plaster around the door had come away! She didn't cry again in the night though. It was very unusual for Dad to shout. Sleep deprivation can do that to a parent sometimes.

When my daughter was younger she sometimes used to wake me up crying after a bad dream. There are not many things worse than that groggy feeling that I got padding from my room into the nursery, although I have never been a big sleeper, the few hours I get need to be of good quality. If she disturbed that, the next day I would be like a dead woman walking. Even losing a small amount of sleep would affect me so it's a good job she didn't require too much attention because I would never have been able to cope. As it happens after she was twelve weeks old she rarely awoke in the night. Not even when she was being potty trained. She did once wake me up to tell me about the most wonderful dream she'd had 'and Father Christmas was in it Mummy, and Rudolph, and Father Christmas was saying "Ho Ho Ho Meeeeerrrry Chrrrrristmas Lucie!". She stood telling me all of this at 3am in the morning in my room with the biggest smile on her face you've ever seen. I couldn't get back to sleep after that for smiling myself. I loved the fact that she had enjoyed herself so much that she couldn't wait until the morning to share it with me. A very treasured and cherished memory!

I didn't want to go to school that day but I knew I wouldn't be able to get out of it, I wasn't poorly. So despite my biggest protests I got into my school uniform. They didn't look any different, they were the same clothes I had been putting on over the last few months since I started my primary school but I felt different. I loved my school uniform. I had a pleated pinafore dress, with a fresh crisp white shirt underneath and a bright red tie. My blazer was grey with a red rim all the way around the collar. It reminded me of the Ready Brek advert where the kids would walk to school surrounded by the orange glow. I had a variety of socks and tights, red ones, white ones, long, short, but it was the pleats on the pinafore I loved best. They made me feel grown up like my Mum and my sister. Grace had worn this uniform first obviously but I didn't mind getting her hand me downs. Quite often Mum used to buy us the same outfits anyway, so mine lasted twice as long as Grace's because I grew out of mine into hers. But I never minded. Grace was always so beautiful in everything it made me feel close to her to wear her things.

At school I was in the Reception class with a lady called Janet Grainger. Mrs Grainger was the nicest teacher that could ever be in a primary school. She had so much enthusiasm about her. She developed and nurtured each child with the passion that I wish and believe every teacher should have. She is the reason why, for a long while, I wanted to be a primary school teacher. Unfortunately it has become too much about the paperwork and achievement figures now rather than developing a child's imagination, that's what I'm good at. Paperwork is something that just doesn't excite me.

I don't remember what I learnt that day, I don't recall what I did in the classroom, however, I do remember climbing up the A-frame in the playground and seeing how far I could see. As long as I could recall I had been a bit of a dare devil. I think because I adored my Dad so much I had secretly turned into a raging tomboy. I stood at the top of the frame looking over the fence outside the school. All I wanted was to be at home even though I knew Dad wasn't there. Instead I was looking into the gardens of the houses to the right of our school. They were massive houses. One of them had a big tree house in the back. A properly built tree house, with an entrance door and a roof with little eaves hanging down. 'I could go there' I thought to myself, 'when the police come for me, they wouldn't find me there.' I had my plan now. I wouldn't tell but I knew where I could run to if someone found out. And to get there I wouldn't have to cross any roads, which I wasn't allowed to do on my own, so Mummy wouldn't be more cross with me. I could just sneak down the side passage and cut through the hedge into the garden. No one would see me. It never crossed my mind that there would be children in the house, that played in that tree house. In my mind I had built my own little world for me and Pinky in there. We'd be safe in our little universe.

When the bell rang I didn't want to come down from there. I felt so free, as though I were on top of the world.

Mum picked me up from school as normal and I went to play in my bedroom but I couldn't concentrate on anything much so I sat in front of the window watching the old oak tree we had in our back garden. The back garden was long and narrow with very few plants or flowers in. The house was three windows wide at the back and the garden must have extended about 30 feet beyond the house. All the way around the footings of our house were patio flags creating a little path, and the grass was always really lush and green because Dad cared for it so well. There was a fence between our house and the Granolli's next door and a small passageway which didn't lead anywhere, except our pet cemetery, in between the two houses. Where the pet cemetery was there was no grass but the earth was moist and mossy. It always smelt great down there. Damp and warm. Grace once disappeared for ages and Mum and Dad couldn't find her. They eventually found her down the side of the house with her bucket and spade. She was digging up the goldfish we had buried about three weeks before to "check it was ok". The rabbit we had was buried down there along with several hundred goldfish (which I only found out recently as I thought we had two goldfish in our childhood, Goldie and Squish). Apparently, on discovering a dead one, Dad used to rush home with a new one whilst Mum kept us away from the tank. I always had Squish. I thought Goldie was a really glamorous name. It suited Grace's fish. Mine was always the fat one which would eat all the food, hence the name Squish.

The garden went really far out to the side and we had a shed just at the foot of the oak tree. Sukey got stuck up the tree by her collar once. I remember being so upset to find the cat hanging. Dad went up the ladder and lifted her down. That was the last time she ever wore a collar. Mum decided because she was a stray cat she wasn't used to it so it wasn't really fair.

The old oak tree was really hard to climb because there must have been about seven or eight feet of trunk before any branches started, however to us being so small it felt like 30 feet. I loved the acorns it used to drop in the Autumn and the rustle of the leaves that I would hear whilst I was in bed and it was stormy outside. There were always squirrels in our garden because of the old oak tree, gatherings up nuts for the winter. About half way up there was a hollow in the trunk which I would imagine a wise old owl lived in. Particularly when I read the book 'The Owl Who Was Afraid of the Dark', which was one of my favourite books. I could picture the story revolving around our tree with all the local animals taking the parts of the other characters. I was devastated recently when I went back to see the close we lived in and they had cut it down. All that history from my family, and the families before us, gone. It felt like losing part of my heritage.

The buds were starting to form on the branches and I knew that in a matter of weeks when the tree would be full of leaves they would dance in the wind on a day like today.

I loved sitting at the window looking at the outside. Sundays with Dad had given me a love of nature and all things living, to watch the birds fly by and the animals in the garden just going about their daily business was one of my favourite things to do.

Besides, the windowsill was where the fairies came through if you lost a tooth. I had written to them once. I made sure I'd asked all the questions I wanted to know about, you know what were their names? Where did they live? How old were they? I even left a tiny pencil. It was from Wales, one of those massive ones, you could get from any seaside pier, with a little piece of gold string attached to a plastic package at the top with 5 tiny pencils in. I left them one of those to write with, you know, just to make it easier. I left it all on the windowsill and my tooth under my pillow wrapped in a piece of tissue and sure enough in the morning there was a shiny twenty pence piece and my note. The fairy was called Tinkerbell and she lived at the bottom of the garden. She'd had so many birthdays she didn't know how old she was but she was a kind and good fairy and she was glad I looked after my teeth well.

Once, when I lost a tooth, I had taken it to the sink to give it a last minute clean before I wrapped it up in the usual piece of tissue and placed it under my pillow for the tooth fairies. The tissue was ready to go on the side and I was scrubbing away with my toothbrush to make it gleam so I would get a good coin from them. But I dropped it down the plug hole. I was devastated. Aunty Sandra and Uncle Andrew were over for the day and, bless my Aunty Sandra, she went outside and got on her hands and knees putting her hand down the drain to see if she could find it for me. She sat there with her hands covered in crap from down the drain. We couldn't find it but seeing her there, trying so hard to make it better, made me stop crying. I left a note for the fairies that night too telling them what had happened and sat in bed waiting to hear if they came. I fell asleep at some point, tiredness took over from my anxiety, and sure enough in the morning my shiny twenty pence piece was there. That gives you an idea of the type of family I come from. They would do anything to make anyone happy.

Grace was playing in the garden with Moira and Marie from next door. I could hear them giggling but I didn't want to go and join in. I didn't want to laugh because if I laughed my secret might come out. I desperately wanted to keep this one. I wasn't very good at keeping secrets, particularly not important ones. I always got far too excited and ended up telling the person I had something to tell. This one was different. I didn't like this one.

The tree was blowing gently and the sun moved behind the clouds. It was almost ironic, this beautiful sunny day ruined, tainted by my dark mood.

The next time Nana and Granddad came over it felt different. I stuck to my Dad's side like a limpet. As soon as they came I became my Dad's shadow, much to his annoyance I didn't want him out of my sight. When I was finally sent out to play with Grace I lay on the front garden underneath the cherry blossom tree looking through the window. Would he tell them? I felt unclean. I wanted to wash my hands. I wanted a bath. Even in my nightmares I'd never felt this much fear. I was sure my friends must know. They all looked so happy and carefree. I couldn't understand why if there were such things as naughty children's places, they could be so lackadaisical about everything. Weren't they scared of the police? Weren't they worried about their sins? Perhaps it was just me? Perhaps I was the only one who was naughty. Perhaps there weren't many children in these homes, they were just for special girls like me.

I decided to move away from the window and got my bike out as I had a million times before when they'd come over. As I would for the next two years of living in this house each time. I'd take myself off to play in my friends' worlds which seemed a bit better than mine. If I tried really hard I could imagine that everything was fine. I was all right. I was clean. I became adept at pretending, living in my own fantasy world. My daydreams became so vivid it sometimes became hard to distinguish between them and the reality. I was turning myself inward and setting the foundations for a lifetime of feeling a sense of not belonging or knowing what to do when I went to any place new. Part of me was scared to get settled into home because I knew that there was always that threat there. I knew the police could come at any time.

Next time I went to stay at Nana's house I stuck to her like glue. Grace was staying too. She was getting to the age where she didn't want to sleep in the same room as me because she wanted some privacy. She slept in the front room now. The front bedroom was prettier because it looked out over the road and the pretty flowers at the front, not that we could ever have the windows open. The area was too dangerous for us to do that. There were many stories about people having their back door open and someone knocking on the front door, keeping the owner talking whilst their house was burgled. Granddad installed a fake alarm box on the front with wires going into the house. I never knew why he put wires on it because they normally didn't have them. I think he'd thought he was being clever, outsmarting the criminals.

We went shopping with Nana to the market. There was a pub was at the top of the road she had lived on for what seemed like forever to me. It was my favourite part of the walk into Civic Centre because it had a high brick wall and Nana would hold my hand as I walked along. She always held my hand really tightly because on the other side of the wall there was loads of glass from when the revellers came out after having a few too many. Then at the entrance to the pub there was a separate area where the wall created a raised circular platform. It became a dare to jump from the wall to the platform and then run round it as fast as you could. Then move onto the next wall which led to a really sharp bush that you had to jump down before you got near to it. Nana took me into Civic past the jewellers, past the post office, round into the precinct and through the walkway to the market. The market had always fascinated me because of the diversity of people who were there. There were the older generation, a million look-a-likes of my Nana and Granddad, the ladies in their head scarves, the men in their flat caps. All the older ladies had trolleys so they could carry their shopping with ease. Then there were the younger kids, they can only have been in their early teens, all scruffy but cool looking. Standing on corners, smoking and swearing. It was an eye opener for someone as young as me. I had heard many stories about how they mugged the old ladies they saw on their own so I held on even tighter to Nana's hand protectively as we rounded the cut through to the market. All the stalls fascinated me. The people behind them all looked so cheerful in this dismal setting. Nana wanted to show us off to everybody she saw. Everybody told Grace how like her Dad she looked. Nobody spoke to me really apart from to say hello or ruffle my hair and smile.

On the way home as we ate our sweets from the best sweetshop in the world Nana told us a story about when my Mum was little. She had been walking down that very same route on her way home from the shops, when something caught her eye. Tucked into the hedge of one of the first houses you came to was a one pound note. She'd picked it up and ran home. They decided they were going to go to Llandudno on the train because that would be a real treat. It wouldn't be something they could afford to do again because nobody had a spare pound in those days. I marveled at how much a pound would have bought for you. I was just beginning to understand the value of money because of the tooth fairies and I knew what my twenty pence could buy me. I could go into the bakery in Bramhall village and get a raw bun (bread roll) as I called them and still have enough money to buy a mix bag and a quarter of my favourite sweets. Or a Striper bar or a Wham bar. They were the best! Wham bars! They were jaw breakers. You had to suck them until they softened in your mouth and became gooey enough to bite them then chew. If they were soft enough they would stretch out to be three or four times the length when you bit them and you could curl the thinner piece up onto your tongue, your mouth bulging with sugar. However, if you started to chew before it was soft enough your jaw would ache and you would be picking bits out of your teeth for hours afterwards. Refreshers were the same, not the ones that were crumbly in the packet but the chewy sweets. I liked Refreshers, they lasted for ages in your mouth and made your tongue feel all sticky.

As we approached the shadow of the tree at the front of the house, it felt like the onset of my own private darkness and my fear returned. I'd left it at the gate as we had walked away from the house, but it had waited here for me. The sun was low in the sky for the morning and hidden behind the house. The path littered with bits of crisps packets, sweet wrappers and me. My legs felt heavier as I approached the front door. I wasn't sure if he would be at the Legion or at home. I knew the drinking would have begun.

Mum once told me that he was very cruel to Nana but I hadn't seen this. Maybe it was the drink, maybe it was something else because to me he always seemed to love her although they weren't very demonstrative together and they slept in separate beds which seemed silly because they were married. All grown ups slept in bigger beds. Even my Mum and Dad. I thought that when you got married you went to the bigger bed company and they would ask to see you were married before sending out the new big bed to your house. I couldn't imagine ever wanting to sleep in a bed with Nana though. She snored really loudly, so loudly in fact I could hear her through the wall at night.

The house was quiet and cool. He wasn't here. I rushed into the living room to see my bear. I hadn't seen him for a while. He still smiled back at me, his head cocked to one side. He seemed to have a softer face today. Grace came in and took him off me. She wanted him. I was sad. He was my bear. He kept my secrets. A while later when she had finished playing with him and I stood in the kitchen with my fingers curled around him, I felt better.

In the kitchen there was an old fashioned washing machine tucked into a little alcove just as you walked through the door on the left hand side. It was one of those ones which had a door on the top and made a terrible racket when it was spinning. Because the house didn't have central heating Nana had a clothes rack that pulled down from the high ceiling over the kitchen table. She was loading clothes whilst making a cup of tea. She had one of those old kettles that you popped onto the stove and which whistled when the water was boiling. She always made the nicest pots of tea and let us have as much sugar in them as we wanted. Her sugar was always set out on the table in a shiny silver bowl with a square spoon in it that looked like an old coal shovel, just tiny.

As the day went on I relaxed more. Maybe I was ok here? Was it all a dream? Some of my daydreams had become so real I couldn't remember which were true and which weren't. He came home from the Legion staggering slightly, his nose was red, and we sat down to tea at the table. He seemed to be back to normal Granddad, in high spirits and joking about all the regulars in the Legion. He checked on his wine after tea which was happily bubbling away into the S shaped tube at the top of the huge glass bottle over in the corner of the room and talked to Grace and I about how it was made. Strange really how two girls so young would know everything there was to know about fermentation. There was always an open bottle of wine in their fridge with a hand written label on to show what it was made from. The more he talked to us the more I began to think it was a dream. It had been quite a while since I last came over and time seemed to have made it better.

After tea Nana bathed us and we joined Granddad in the living room. Nana was putting her rollers in, as she did every night and Granddad was sat on the sofa with a drink in his hand.

'Let me scratch your back popsy' he said. I froze. Surely he couldn't scratch my back now.

'Come on Rachy' he said. I moved slowly over to sit in front of him as he asked Nana to pass the scratcher. He loosened the towel slightly that I had up to my neck and started to very gently scratch my back. I sat stiff as a board. But he just carried on scratching my back and watching the television. I could smell the alcohol on his breath and I knew he was drunk. Grace was getting into her pyjamas behind the chair to preserve her dignity. She had started to get shy about herself, even in the bath. She used to wear a bikini if she could. In a jiffy she was changed and Nana was brushing her hair. Now it was my turn. I stood up and walked to behind the chair. He was still just watching television smiling away in his drunken state. When I was in my nightie I felt better, more comfortable. He looked at me with a peculiar look on his face. Grace was sitting at Nana's feet passing her the rollers one by one.

I remember one time when Nana had put rollers into my hair before bed. I had slept terribly but when they came out in the morning I had the most glorious curls in my naturally straight hair. I felt like a princess for a day although they probably dropped out within about five minutes. I still felt glamorous. I had gone into Nana's jewellery box and got out mounds of necklaces, bracelets and tried them on walking up and down in her bedroom looking at myself in the mirror on her dressing table. The room always smelt a little bit musty and there were wires taped to the carpet that went to the plug sockets in the wall from their electric blankets. I felt like a movie star! Swishing along in all my jewels, finery, my curly hair and Nana's fur coat!

At 7.30pm it was time for bed and Grace and I climbed the stairs, said goodnight to each other and went our separate ways. I drifted in and out of a dozing sleep. I was tired tonight and the weight of the covers seemed to be pulling me down into a deeper sleep than I got at home. When I woke up I could hear Nana snoring in her room and I knew that everywhere downstairs was locked up because the house was silent. I snuggled into Pinky, into that smell of home that was always on his ear.

Planes were still taxiing on the runway and I started to think about the noises that the engines made. I must have dozed off again because the next time I awoke it was to see him stood at the door. He couldn't see my eyes I don't think, maybe he'd come to change the potty. I kept my eyes as tightly shut as I could praying that my heart in my throat wasn't pounding as loud as it felt to be. I heard him as he crept across the carpet and I felt him start to tug the covers away from the side of the bed. Nana was still snoring.

My hands felt dirty. I wanted to be clean. I was scared.

His warmth crept under the cold covers with me and he seemed to be fumbling with something. All the while he was whispering to me, into my hair. 'Special girl. My little virgin arse. Come on now to Gramps'. His moustache was rough and felt like Velcro attached to my head, but I still kept my eyes tightly closed. I could feel his hand on the top of my leg pulling my nightie closer. I was angled slightly facing away towards the wall with Pinky held tightly to my nose so I couldn't smell him. My bear was downstairs, I bet he was playing the piano and smiling now. I could almost hear the sweet music as Granddad slid his hands into my pants feeling around for my bottom. I must have stirred slightly because he knew I was awake. 'Wake up popsy. Gramps wants some virgin arse.' he said. The pain I felt as he slipped his finger in my bottom was excruciating. I stared at the wall as the silent tears fell down my cheeks, but I didn't grimace. I looked at the window which I could see down the side of the curtains. And all the while planes were taking off outside. I could just about see the lights as they swooped around in circles before plunging themselves into darkness as they set off on their journey to far off lands. He moved my hand to on top of his penis as he pushed into my bottom deeper. My hands were dirty. He opened the front pocket in his pyjamas and took out his penis. He'd always worn the kind that were two tone in either dark brown and light brown or the same in blue. He was sliding my knickers down with his other hand just so they sat on the edge of my bottom. I turned Pinky away I didn't want him to see this. He might change the way he felt about me. Granddad moved my hand from his penis. It had felt small when he first came in but now it felt bigger.

He curled his hand around the front of my chin holding onto my mouth. It was the hand that had been in my bottom. I felt sick building up in my throat. I could smell something on his hand. Was it my bottom? It was on my face.

My lips felt sticky with the sweat from his hand and my hands from him. As he jerked inside me from behind I looked at the window. My body was crushed against the wall, against Pinky. Pinky knew now. Even though he couldn't see me because he was facing the wall he was spooned between me. I was almost doing the same to him as Granddad was doing to me.

The outside of the windowsill was lit up by the street lamps that stood tall throughout the little community of old peoples homes that stood behind their house, 172.

The paint on the windowsill was slightly peeling and I found if I looked at it hard enough that I could see all the cracks around the peel. There were seven in all, all leading off of the same long thin dark line. I was sure he would be able to feel my heart in my throat but I couldn't feel him inside me now. My mind was far away on the window. I could see the old people's home, that was over the back fence. I could see the sweet peas in the back garden, still curling and winding their way up the wire fence. I could see all Nana's beautiful roses and the Canadian number plate hung on the green paint of the garage door in the bottom left hand corner of the garden.

My eyes darted around taking in every detail of the garden, taking in all the colours of the beautiful flowers he cultivated with the same hands that were touching me now. The washing post was leant up against the garden shed and the toys that we had brought with us were outside. It was sunny now.

The garden shed was massive in their garden. It was almost a garage although they had never had a car and it was full of all manner of exciting looking tools and bits of this and that. I loved the smells of paints and turps in there and marveled each time I went in at how organised everything was. I could see it now with all the shelves at the sides and the work bench in the middle. The bike parts, the pots of lotions and potions that Grand-dad used in his crafts, the bits of old wood and all kinds of weird and exciting looking things.

I could imagine Mum playing in here when she was little, feeling the same about all the exciting tubs.

All this I could see from the window next to the cracks in the paint work. All this was in my trance like state and the pain well that was just in my body. I didn't need my body now.

I was awakened by his whisperings and he'd gone quiet now. My bottom felt sticky and gooey. He must have wee'd on me again although I was pleased because it wasn't on my hands this time. He pulled away from my back and reached out of the side of the bed and I heard the trickling of water. I felt a cold flannel being applied to my bottom and then heard him clean himself. I wanted to clean my face but I was too scared to move, too scared to ask. My bum was throbbing and I could feel the pain now. I wasn't at the window anymore, I was there in that dimly lit bedroom. I put my hand to my face to wipe away my quiet tears and I could feel the pattern of the wallpaper embedded on my cheek like the chair pattern from home would be when I nodded off there during the day. He leaned in close to me, his special girl and said 'remember Rachy, our secret. Mummy and Daddy would be cross. They'll send you away if you tell them. They'll hate you.' He didn't have to tell me I knew. I knew I wouldn't tell. I hadn't before and I wouldn't then. 'You won't tell will you' he whispered. I shook my head. The pillow felt wet with my tears. So did Pinky's back. I didn't move for one second as Granddad slid away from me out of the bed. I didn't move when he whispered good night god bless. I didn't move whilst he took his bowl of water and flannel downstairs. I didn't move as he crept back up the stairs back into Nana's bedroom. I don't think I even drew a breath. I heard the lock on Nana's bedroom door go over and what seemed like a few minutes later I heard him start to snore gently. My senses were on red alert. I moved my hand to pull up my pants from the back. It was still damp from the flannel and I was shivering with cold by now. The pocket of warmth I had developed was all gone and my body started to shake violently as warm tears oozed out of the corners of my eyes. I made no sound still. Everything in the house was silent apart from the loud snore of Nana and the faint snore of him.

My whole body ached as I cried and cried. The dim light in the room flickered slightly as it did from time to time. I lay in my bed looking over at the window through tearstained eyes. I couldn't bear to turn Pinky round because he knew. He knew what had happened. I didn't want to see that look in his eyes, same as my bear. Perhaps he wouldn't love me anymore. Perhaps he would smell different, of the alcohol and cheap aftershave that filled my nose. Perhaps he had some of the stickiness on him. I left him facing the wall. Maybe he was on the window too.

I tried to roll onto my back but it was too painful. I lay watching for the sun coming up through the curtains and when Nana got up at around 6.30 I wiped away the last of my tears. I heard her go into the kitchen and pop the kettle on as she always did. I could hear her getting out the bread from the pantry and slicing big doorstep pieces off ready to toast for Grace and I.

I loved Nana's toast. She always put loads of butter on it so it almost melted in your mouth. I could almost smell it now.

I crept out of bed and took my nightie off. I knew that Granddad wouldn't be up for at least another two hours. In my knickers there was a stain, there was a stain and blood. I panicked and threw back the sheets. I couldn't have blood in the bed. I had a great scab on my knee where I had fallen off my bike the week before. I'd sat the day before in the corner of the kitchen floor near Whisky's bowl peeling it up from the outside, picking at each corner until it loosened slightly all over so I could wiggle it gently. I changed my pants and looked down at my leg. I pulled hard at the scab and it came off in one fell swoop. The blood started to come from the middle and round the outside there was a watery liquid, gathering momentum, mixing with the blood that was starting to ooze out onto my now bright red knee. There that could hide it. I slipped my jeans over my sore knee and then my sore bottom. I pulled my vest over my head and down over my body. I was still shaking. I hadn't been able to get warm afterwards so my bones felt cold and achy now. I shoved my soiled knickers into my pocket and tried to make them not stick out. I put the scab from my knee in there too and tiptoed down the stairs in my bare feet. I knew Nana would ask me to get some socks but I didn't care. I wanted to get into the warmth of the kitchen, get the chill away from me. I wanted to go to the toilet. I wanted to get rid of what was inside me so it would be gone. I sat on the loo which was at the bottom of the stairs, as what felt like my stomach fell out. I didn't dare look into the toilet but I looked at the spots of blood on the toilet paper. It wasn't much but it hurt like hell. Every time I wiped it felt like there were a thousand needles digging into my behind. I stood up and pulled up my fresh knickers, the soiled ones still in my pocket and prepared myself for Nana. She was humming in the kitchen and the kettle was whistling. She always listened to GMR radio station because she liked the music that they played. I could never see the point to them because they talked more than they played music. However she loved it and right now it felt familiar and safe to me.

I stuck my head round the door and told her I was going to have a wash. In the bathroom I shut the door, put the plug in and ran the hot tap. I didn't care if I was allowed or not I wanted to clean my hands. I scrubbed and scrubbed at my hands until my eyes fell onto the bowl laying to the side of me in the bath. It was the bowl he had brought up last night. The flannel was spread out over the side of the bath, pure white and clean, but I knew it wasn't.

I could hear Nana putting the grill on. She had one of those old fashioned New World gas cookers that had an open grill at the top. It always made the same noise as it lit. She used really long match sticks to light the top. I loved the smell of burning sulphur as the match lit springing the gas into action mixing with the fresh air, to make my toast, my tasty toast. I stood on my tiptoes to look into the mirror. My face looked tired so I gave it a wash. I knew my toast would be ready in a minute. I buried my skin into the scratchy towel on the rail next to the sink to dry myself off. I took the sink plug out and moved into the kitchen. I could hear Grace stirring above me, at least I thought it was Grace, oh god please don't let it be him.

How could I ever sleep again? How could I take that chance? I was so scared. Bile was building up in my stomach as the wonderful smell of toast drifted across the kitchen. My tummy rumbled, I needed the toilet again. I went, no blood on the toilet tissue this time, it just hurt and it stung when I went. I went back into the kitchen and sat down although I had to sit at an angle because it hurt when I put my bottom cheeks down.

So this is how it was to be from now on. I knew I would never sleep properly again.

I sipped my warm tea as Nana went about her normal morning routine. She was staring out of the window. The same window as the one above that I had stared out of last night. What could she see? What was she thinking whilst she was humming along and tapping her hands in the sink to the music? I know what I was thinking. I wanted my Mum. I wanted my Dad. I wanted my sister. I wanted anyone who didn't smell of alcohol or Old Spice. I wanted Pinky to be normal again. I wanted the bear to smile at me because he liked me not because he knew my secret. I wanted to go home.

Chapter 4

My Imaginary Friend

I threw four pairs of knickers away that weekend. I was gutted because one of them was my favourite pair. They had a picture of a fairy on the front. She was surrounded with, what looked like, little ivy leaves in the shape of a heart. I'd though that that would somehow make it ok, that by throwing them away I could be better, but it didn't. Things would never be ok again. How did other people cope with this, surely I wasn't on my own. There must be other naughty children. Perhaps grown ups could be naughty too. I couldn't imagine Mum and Dad being naughty because that was gross. They didn't do things like that. They were pure. That's why they'd be so mad at me if they knew.

I didn't have the capability to mend inside what was happening to me.

Dad had a box of special dressings called Jellonet squares. They were these lethal but supposedly friendly squares of bandage which had Vaseline spread all over them and ever time Grace or I fell we would be "Dettolled" (the verb to Dettol was used frequently in our house!) in the sink, which hurt more than the cut itself, and then had a Jellonet square applied. He kept them in the first aid box. I had always loved the first aid box because it smelt of Germolene and it was bright red. It was made out of a soft leather look material and had a clasp on the side. The Jellonet squares were kept in a flat turquoise metal container with red tape around the outside. I'm sure they must have been as old as Dad. Problem was with them was that they encompassed the blood of the cut and then the scab grew over the top of them, so by the time you came to peel off the dressing you took the scab right off again. Bloody agony! Some of mine and Grace's best scars have come from Jellonet squares!

How could I fix this though? You couldn't put a Jellonet square on or even see the pain but it was there, granted only for a few days afterwards when my bottom hurt like hell. The pain inside me was the worst bit though. When the physical pain went it left me with a void inside, a blackness, the dark side of the moon, a broken soul! There's no Jellonet square in the world that could mend, so to speak, this. No Dettol could get the grit out of this cut. There were no scars on my body but by God the pain was terrible. Sometimes I would try so hard to find an outlet for my complete and utter confusion that I would scrape my hands, arms or feet on the brick wall outside. Always in a place where no one could see so that I had a physical reason for feeling pain. It felt better when I had blood coming out because I had something physically to look at – a reason. How can you fix a broken soul when you're five and scared? You can't even begin to understand it let alone fix it. It just felt bad.

My childhood was over, and so began a new chapter of my life. I withdrew into myself as much as I possibly could. I tried everything to be accepted with people at school but never felt as though I was. I always loved being on that climbing frame though because there I was free. In my good dreams I had wings and I could fly away from everything. I'd go flying in a warm place around amongst the colourful parrots underneath the sweltering sun, my wings never tiring in my exploration of this strange and beautiful new land. I played holiday memories over and over in my head trying to remember what things I had taken with me and I began to recite my favourite film, Mary Poppins, over and over in my mind to make the bad thoughts go away.

I was once hypnotised in a group therapy course I attended for women who had suffered sexual abuse as children. The lady who was speaking took us across a big valley, passing trees and birds flying towards the other side where there was an opening in the rock. As we walked into the entrance of the tunnel we walked down past doors with the names of people that we knew on until we came to the end of the corridor where there was the door with our name on. I had been enjoying the flight so much that I was far behind everyone else and had to run down the tunnel. That made it feel unsafe, like I was running from something. When I reached my door and opened it up there was nothing there. It was black, dark, scary. The door shut behind me and all I could see was dark. She told us to look around but I couldn't see. She told us to remember what was inside our room because that was what was in our heads. I still saw nothing. Not a light, not a sound, nothing. I was scared. She told us to take a last look and then turn around to go to the door. I span and span looking, searching for the door but it was too dark for me to find the handle. They were walking back up the tunnel and I was still stuck in that room, dark, cold and on my own. When she brought us round I was crying, as were many of the others. We were then given a piece of paper and asked to draw, paint or sketch what we saw in our room. All I could see was black so I painted black. Everybody changed when they saw my picture. I didn't care, I was true to my heart. I was petrified and I wanted to be somewhere bright instead. When they asked who wanted to explain their picture first one of the girls, a pretty lady from Liverpool, wanted me too. It was horrible. I needed to wash my hands again. I washed them every ten minutes for a while, until the black had gone, but it was still there imprinted in my head. I had nothing inside me. Except black.

Outwardly I was a normal young lady, inside I was dying. It was like a cancer, not that I knew what cancer was, eating me inside, spreading taking over my whole being. My smile didn't crack. People commented on my smile a lot. I recall in high school a teacher of mine, Mrs Burton, saying my smile always brightened her day. Until I dyed my hair black that is, when she told me I looked scary. The dye had reacted badly with the perm I had had and gone a smoky blue colour!

So here I was back at my window, back at home, looking out at the stars wishing I really could make my dream come true when out he came. He didn't have a name, my imaginary friend. He didn't have a penis either. Nobody knew about him but me. He loved me. He was the one who would rescue me. I'd imagine us at the park, he would see Gramps and kick his butt! He would know what to do. He would take me away on one of our flights. When the police came to our tree house, we would just stretch our wings out and go off together on our next adventure and if my wings got tired he would take me under his wing and help me. Never stopping to get settled we would fly forever. Far away. In my dream I had the same wallpaper in the escape tree house as in my bedroom, a jungle scene. There were lions, elephants and all manner of animals alongside beautiful green leaves that were shaped like palm trees. In there the animals protected us, me, my friend and Pinky. We were safe. My friend came with me every time I had to go to Nana's house from then on. Nobody knew but he sneaked in when they all looked away. He was handsome in a kind of cute way. He told me stories of how my prince would come and take me away. We would pre-tend I was Rapunzel, locked up in the tower at the window looking down for my rescuer with my long brown locks flowing out of the window. He never knew because I never told him, but he was my prince. He rescued me every time.

Next time I stayed at Nana's when I heard the lock turn on their bed-room door it didn't matter. I was at the window, my friend by my side, looking out over the silky night. Our adventures began.

I felt Granddad's penis in my hand physically, but it wasn't me. I felt him delving into my body, but I wasn't there. I was flying over the house tops of Wythenshawe like the planes I had once loved the sound of. The jerking inside my body didn't matter because I was over the park looking at the strange graffiti that covered every available ledge, sign or bench. I could feel his moustache scratch and irritate my face as he parted my lips, darting his tongue into my mouth like a snake. However, I was over the airport looking down at the big 767 jumbo jet's refuelling for their long journeys.

Once he'd finished I didn't want to come back. It was far more exciting to be out flying, just me and my friend. I felt the stickiness come first, then the cold of the flannel. All the while I didn't say a word. I didn't cry. I didn't whimper. I didn't say a thing. As he cleaned in between my legs I started to shake. He took me in his arms to warm my cold bones. Cold from my trip with my friend. I was coming back from the window as he buried his face into my hair calling me his special girl. Telling me not to worry, that things were ok as long as I didn't tell. He lay with me afterwards for a long time that night, stroking my face, chuckling under my chin. He didn't have to touch me, his fingerprints were all over me anyway. I could feel him from home. His hands exploring parts of my body that I didn't want him to. I didn't need him in this bed. It used to be my bed at Nana's, now it wasn't. I didn't want it. I wanted it to burn. I wanted him to burn.

I was back there now. In that bed. I could see my friend on the window sill. He looked sad like he wanted me to play with him instead. He snarled at Granddad who of course didn't see him, but I loved him more for doing it, for trying to protect me.

Granddad started to doze off. I didn't want to move unless I woke him but my arm was stuck underneath him and he had his hand around my shoulder on top of my chest. I didn't like him to touch my chest. It felt funny.

He eventually did wake up and move, but by then my arm was so pale, dead that I couldn't feel it properly for the rest of the night. Nana's snoring went on as he crept away from me to pop the bowl downstairs and as he jumped back into his bed to drop into his satisfied slumber.

I'd done it! I'd survived it! I wasn't there when it happened, I was away flying. My body ached but my mind felt free. I closed my eyes and drifted off to sleep dreaming about my friend and our flying adventure. There was no blood in the morning on my sheets which was good because I had no scabs to pick to explain it away. After I'd had my toast with Nana first thing the phone rang. They had a phone in the kitchen, it was a proper dial phone with their number written on in his writing. The box bit was a beige colour whilst the handset a deep brown colour. I always loved holding the receiver down whilst I dialled imaginary numbers and had conversations with people from all over the world. I liked the way that the dial swished back after it got to the bar that made it register the number.

It was Mum, she talked to me for a while and then told me they wouldn't be coming for me until the day after. Panic set in! I'd done it last night. How could I do it again? All day I couldn't concentrate, not even with the jolly lady on the best sweet stall, not on the wall outside the pub at the top of Nana's road, not on the garlic sausage that Nana bought to make my lunch with on milk roll. My food seemed stuck in my throat not wanting to go down into my stomach for fear of it being thrown straight back up.

As I watched him drink more and more watching my every move I knew I had to prepare. I knew that I needed to switch off. I needed to try to sleep through but I also knew I couldn't. Try as I may I couldn't get off. I lay in the dimly lit room listening, waiting, for I knew he would come. Pinky faced the wall, even his smell couldn't comfort me tonight. He knew I was sad, I'd seen it in his eyes before I turned him away. He knew I was scared. I could see my friend at the window, watching, waiting for me but I couldn't get there.

I heard the lock on their bedroom door slide over and the handle start to turn before anything. I shut my eyes tight to try to get out of my body and away but I couldn't. I don't know why.

His movements were stealth like going down the stairs to get his cleansing equipment. His ritual was beginning.

I felt him opening the covers that Nana had tightly tucked in, after taking my hot water bottle out of the bed, to keep in the warmth. 'How's my Rachy' he slurred. 'Ready for some of me. Ready to take it all. Plans, plans I've got plans Rachy. You are gonna make me feel so good little Virgin. So good. C'mon baby, Gramps needs a cuddle.'

My eyes looked up at him, they must have been filled with fear. But he either didn't see it or he didn't care. His penis was already out, it had been out as he had walked towards me, angry and dark coloured pointing from side to side as he walked across the shadowed room. 'You want some don't you' he said.

As he stroked my hair with his hand and started to bring me down towards his penis I knew he wanted me to suck it like a lollipop. He coaxed it into my mouth and I gagged. He tightened the grip on my hair forcing me up and down on top of it. He pushed into my mouth and it touched my tonsils making me gag and gasp for air, tears streaming down my face. With his other hand he was feeling into my knickers, touching me, tainting me. I felt everything in my mind, this was wrong. He slid one of his fingers up my bottom and one in where I wee'd from. Oh god the pain. I wanted to be sick, I wanted the toilet. He told me I felt full and asked had I been to the toilet today. I couldn't reply because I had my mouth around the penis. He pulled my head back to make me reply. As he did he jerked his fingers out from inside me. It felt like I was being ripped apart, inside out. The potty was over there and he wanted me to empty myself, he wanted me to sit there and get everything out of me. I ask if I could go to the toilet to do it but he said no he wanted to watch me. I crouched over the potty and began to squeeze. My bottom was throbbing because his finger had been in there. He was wiping it off onto the clean flannel as I strained to get the day's food out from inside my belly. When I knew I couldn't do anymore he asked me to stand up. He didn't mind that I hadn't wiped, he didn't care that I wasn't clean . I wasn't clean anyway. He sat on the side of the bed with his legs open. His penis was pointing up at me. I thought he wanted me to suck it again but he didn't. He turned me around so I was facing the inside wall of the house and asked me to sit on his knee. He had one of his hands on the base of my back and the other tucked under my chin as he eased his penis inside me. I was pleased though because I couldn't smell my waste on his hands tonight. It was a victory, a small victory. He was moving me up and down on it as my silent tears rolled down my face wetting his hand under my chin. 'Take it Rachy, come one take it'. Bile rose into my throat but I swallowed it down. My feet were on the ground but only my toes touched now as I tried to pull further away from his pulsing but he didn't let me. He wanted me to split in two. His hand were pushing me, pulling me, pushing me, pulling me, making me feel more and more seasick. I wanted to be at the window but instead all I could do was look for my friend. He wasn't there, he'd gone, where had he gone? Was he flying without me? Had he found another naughty girl to help escape?

Granddad stuck me with it, again and again inside me and I felt his body tensing, his breathing getting heavier, heavier. Then he juddered to a stop. My bottom was agony as he lifted me up to sit me on his knee, properly this time, as a Granddad should.

'Now then popsy, a chat I think. You know how Gramps likes you to have an empty arse, from now on you go to the toilet before bed, do you hear me.' I nodded at him through my tear filled eyes. 'If you don't I'll tell' he said. This time he saw the fear. 'I'm sorry poppet, I won't tell, not if you promise to be a good girl and do as you're told'. He rocked me in his arms all the time talking to me in a soothing voice. And it felt strangely nice. This was the part of him I loved. The part that could make it better. Stroking my face.

The stickiness leaking from my bottom onto his knee brought me back to the other half of him, but he didn't seem to mind. He lay me on the bed facing the wall as he began his clean up mission. The water had gone cold, colder than it had been before, because he'd been here forever.

My friend was back. He was watching me with a sad look in his eyes. Whispering to me "it's almost done, it's almost over". I buried my nose into Pinky to get rid of the smells. It smelt dirty in the room now, dirty and dangerous. Granddad tucked the sheets around me, kissed me on the head and moved off towards the door. My nose was running so badly now that I wiped the sleeve of my nightie across my face. It was my favourite nightie. It had a picture of Sad Sam on the front. I knew now how Sad Sam felt. I know why he had sad eyes. I had sad eyes too. And it was over. He was gone.

I didn't want to fly with my friend now. I just wanted to cry myself to sleep. I needed him to stay with me. He did. He stroked my hair and the side of my face like Mum did at night when I couldn't sleep. He made me safe. A safe and sound girl again I drifted off to sleep.

It wasn't a good sleep that night but I didn't care. I was going home that day. My friend and I sat at the window in the living room waiting for Mum and Dad to come for me. Mike came after church before Mum and Dad. He hugged me and called me poppet like he always did. He was a man he must have a penis. Did he want the same from me? He didn't seem to. He was just happy throwing me up in the air and making me giggle until a different kind of tear fell down the sides of my cheeks.

I flung myself at my Dad when he arrived. My safety was here. My hero, after of course now, my imaginary friend.

At home later in the safety of my own bed I talked to my friend about what had happened. I wanted to know why I couldn't get to the window. Why he had gone. He said he didn't like watching. He said I needed not to look at the door for him coming in, that I needed to focus on the window. He held me in his arms and he stroked my hair, just like Gramps had after he changed from Granddad to Gramps. But it felt good. I decided that Granddad was Granddad when I was just the body and Gramps when he wasn't frightening me. It became easier to think of him like that, as two people. I could see him like the market stall owners saw his. Like the men down at the Legion. Like Mike saw him. Like Nana saw him.

My friend promised me he had found somewhere exciting to take me when I was ready. I decided I just wanted to sleep that night because I was so tired after the lack of sleep I had had. So he said he would stay with me until I went to sleep and that he would guard me whilst I rested. He wouldn't let anyone near. He would beat them up if they came to try. He would warn me if the police came. He would protect me. I feel asleep soon after. I couldn't bear to have any part of my body showing from the covers after that. It is something that I find very hard to do now, sleep with any part of my body exposed. Even in the summer, when I get so hot underneath the duvet that I have nightmares.

I hid deep beneath the covers with only my face showing, my duvet tucked firmly underneath my chin, facing the window. I was ready to go at a moments notice. I never turned away from that window for a second, not even in my sleep.

I never woke up again over the next few months without my friend being there. He gave my something that no one else could give. He gave me peace at night.

Christmas was fast approaching now. A year seemed to last an eternity to me as a child. They fly by now, but back then it seemed like forever between my birthday and Christmas Day.

I've always loved Christmas. I love giving people the presents I've chosen for them. I hate my birthday but I love Christmas. I start my Christmas shopping so early that the previous one has barely gone but it's because I love that festive feeling. It makes me feel clean, safe, pure.

Perhaps the purity was to do with the religion we were taught in school. I had had a solo part in the nativity play. I remember when they were trying to pick the person to sing the solo I wanted it so badly that I sat up straighter than everyone else, I sang louder, I smiled more than anyone and I got the part. I was so my own best friend! I learnt my lines faithfully right up until the last minute and as I started singing I knew Mum and Dad were there, and their friends, and Mrs Grainger and Mrs Wardell my next teacher, and they were all watching me singing in this dark room, but I didn't care. This was my moment of glory in the spot light. I sang like an angel, about angels ironically, visiting the Virgin Mary. I was really nervous as I sang and started to fiddle with the bottom of my dress, rolling it up. By the time I got to the end of my song I had rolled the dress right up to my vest and all you could see according to my Mum was a pair of knickers tucked inside a bright white vest, big socks and nobbly, bruised knees. Apparently there wasn't a dry eye in the house.

Another thing my friend helped me with was Christmas. He said he would speak to Father Christmas for me. When we went to see Santa at a meeting of Dad's work friends I was desperate to ask him if my friend had spoken to him but I didn't dare in case he hadn't

One of the things that scared me most was that I would get nothing, because I knew that only good girls and boys got presents from Father Christmas. Grace and I still left the carrot for Rudolph and the glass of sherry, in one of the posh glasses from the dresser cupboard in the dining room and a mince pie for him. The sherry glasses were tall and tinged blue with a gold rim around the top. I used to imagine it would be the kind of glass the Queen drank her milk out of because it was so grand yet dainty and delicate as only a Queen would use. I didn't like the smell of the sherry but Mum's mince pies always smelt good, although I didn't like the taste of them.

I wondered did Santa have a penis. Was that how he knew that girls were naughty or nice. He'd asked me to sit on his knee as well. But he didn't put his inside me.

I'm sure he could read minds as well as hearing from my parents whether I'd been good. I wondered if he spoke to Grandparents as well? I must have been ok though during the year, because on Christmas morning when we rushed down the stairs to the sounds of Dad shouting 'He's been' and threw open the door there was a huge mountain of presents in my Santa sack. We spent what felt like hours ripping open the brightly coloured papers as a family, just the four of us, music playing in the background on the stereo separates in the dining room.

We nipped to see Nana and Gramps before going off to see Dad's family for Christmas lunch as we normally did. Gramps was Gramps that day. It was perfect. As Mum and Dad loaded Grace and I into the car at night half asleep I was actually happy. I couldn't be that much of a naughty girl really if I could have this much at Christmas. Maybe by not telling I'd made it ok. Maybe it was all going to be ok from now on.

I'd thought at Christmas that everything would be fine from then on. I was very wrong. I thought that things would return back to normal because if Father Christmas had known I was really a good girl, how could he be wrong?

Chapter 5

Adventures at the Window

The next time I stayed was on my own and Nana let me sleep in the front room. The front room was prettier, the bed was in the middle of the room and had a flowery over sheet on it. I knew he was coming because I'd heard the lock on Nana's door turn. I had almost felt his footprints coming towards me. I knew it was the middle of the night because the streetlamps had gone off taking away the shadows from the old horse chestnut tree in the front garden and the house was dark apart from the dim landing light. When I say landing it wasn't like my landing at home which was spacious and curled around the top of the stairs, it was a four-foot square of carpet at the top of the stairs. It was like everything in that house, dark and gloomy. It led to the stairs, which were steeper than ours at home, and had a rail that ran either side that my sister and I used to hold onto with our arms locked tight and swing our legs down over the stairs for hours at a time or until Nana or Gramps caught us when we'd get shouted at because they thought we would fall. We never did mind, always watching each other's back carefully, one or the other keeping nit and ready to save in a flash if their was an accident going to happen.

I'd already decided that I didn't like the prettier room at night as much as the back room even though during the day I'd loved it. The shadows from the tree dancing across my window weren't familiar and I couldn't see down the side of the curtains to the window with the bed being in the middle of the room.

He uncurled the covers from around the side of the bed and reached into my body. I wasn't there though. I was pulling the curtains open to let in the light of the day. My friend and I were climbing down the drainpipe at the front of the house and we were running along the road, almost skipping towards the park, as he cupped his hand around my chin and touched my puppy fat chest. We passed the spot where Nana had found the pound note, turned left past the pub and I jumped from the wall to the circle like I'd never jumped before. I was invincible! We ran through the market past the cool kids, ignoring all the people, just running and laughing through the gloomy greyness of it all. As the penis was in my hand and Granddad was kissing my hair I was running over the green of Civic Centre playing catch with my friend and he couldn't catch me. I was faster, stronger, better than I had ever been before. I jerked this way and that way with both my Granddad physically and my friend in my game of tick. He still couldn't catch me. I was the champion of the world. My hair was streaming out behind me as I ran and ran, my friend calling out to his Rapunzel and he caught me! The pain seared through my body, I had been enjoying my self so much that I wasn't prepared for the way I would jolt back. I wanted to be swirled in the air like a leaf on a breeze by my imaginary friend, but instead I was here in this unfamiliar room with Granddad and I was scared, alone, confused and it hurt like hell.

Tears rolled down the sides of my cheeks. Granddad was smiling as he looked into my eyes. 'Why can't he see my pain' I thought. As if I'd made him his face changed. He softened. A look of concern crossed his eyes. 'Don't say it Granddad', I said 'I won't tell, please just don't say it!'. I was almost sobbing now, whilst Nana snored away in the next room.

After his cleaning ritual was done he snuggled into bed with me kissing my hair calling me his special girl, but he didn't threaten me that night. I lay in Gramps's arms, the Gramps that I loved, who just wanted to comfort me as if the last half an hour had been a dream, a terrible, shattering, sick, twisted dream. All the time he held me he was calm. I had my head on his chest and could hear his heart thumping through his brown pyjamas. Thud! Thud! Thud! Almost in time with Nana's snore. His warmth had started to seep through to me and although I could smell the alcohol on his breath I wasn't scared anymore, I didn't feel safe but I wasn't scared. I knew Granddad had gone and Gramps was looking after me now.

It was really hard to distinguish between the two by just looking, but in attitude I knew. I'd grown to accept that this would just happen. Things happened in the dark, things happened in the light, things happened that were dark, secret, but I knew I could keep my secret. My secret enabled me still to have my Gramps, whom I loved very dearly. My anger was all directed at Granddad and subsequently the dark.

So many things happened in the dark. Sometimes it was so black I think I've chosen not to remember, but occasionally I'll wake up in the middle of the night, in a sweat, having been somewhere in my dreams that I never, ever want to revisit and I know it's not just been a dream but a flashback. I started to have a reoccurring dream where I was locked in a dark room with Granddad, I knew he was coming but I didn't know what angle from. I felt him all around me. His hand would touch my back or my leg or my arm and I would be crying, silently. If the light was there I don't think I would have cried in my dream, but it wasn't. I often woke up to real tears slipping down my face or screamed and woke Mum and Dad up.

Winter left taking the coldness away. Not even the light nights of spring could make me feel better.

The blossom appeared on the tree in the front garden early that year. The spring had been warm. My sixth birthday, came and went, another thousand daydreams, another thousand adventures on my windowsill.

I would sit under the blossom tree in the front garden looking in through the large window at the front of the house each time Nana and Gramps came to visit praying to God that he wouldn't tell anyone I was naughty. He never did. He was Gramps when he came to my house. I still sat outside though under the tree, whilst the blossom petals fell like confetti around my head.

I loved the blossom petals. I used to daydream that it was confetti on my wedding day. I was marrying my imaginary friend with no penis. He looked so handsome in his suit with his thick blonde hair, broad shoulders and his safe eyes. He smiled at me as I walked up the aisle towards him in my beautiful white dress and ballet slippers. He was my saviour. He knew everything and he didn't think I was bad. He was always himself, exactly as I wanted him.

My life revolved around the nearest window. It was my escape in adventure land or 'Rachland' as I now call it. In my adventures I could fly, skate, run, jump, do anything to get away from Granddad. I had my tree house where I was safe. In my daydreams I had a Gramps who loved me for being me and not for being the special naughty girl I had become.

I still cried myself to sleep at night silently wishing away the darkness. Mum and Dad always left the landing light on so the bulb shone into my face, but it still wasn't light enough for me. The dark was a source of terror. My night terror. I frequently screamed in my sleep, particularly if I stayed at one of my friends houses as the room wouldn't be familiar to me and their parents wouldn't leave a light on. Mum had to warn everyone I stayed with. I used to wait until the first light of morning before I would shut my eyes. Consequently I was always tired. In my room though I was safe and if it all got too much I would simply ask Mum to take me to bed. She used to tell me stories about a doll called Buttercup and her adventures with her owner, Jennifer Jones. Then Dad would always come up and tuck me in. He'd moved onto asking me questions about countries, their capital cities and currencies and I always tried to persuade him to stay for just two more questions.

I used to creep into Mum and Dad's bed in the middle of the night when I could get away with it. I always got in with my Dad on his side. He was warm and he smelt safe. He used to wrap his arms around me and I knew no one could touch me there and then. If I lay really quiet I could stay there all night snuggled up in his warmth but if I moved he would realise I was still there and I would be taken back into my own room into the cold darkness.

Mum and Dad had wooden slatted wardrobes in their bedroom. The doors had always given me the creeps at night but during the day I loved looking through them at Mum's glamorous clothes. She had so many things in different bright colours. I always wanted to be like her when I grew up and have wardrobes full of shiny tops, trousers and skirts. She had jewellery as well, in little boxes scattered over the dressing table. I used to love looking through them, playing with beads and chains, whilst inhaling all the familiar smells of my parents.

It was around that age that I found out that if you were ill you didn't have to go to school and got to spend the day at home with Mum. I started to pretend all the time that I was ill. I would secretly sneak into Mum and Dad's bedroom whilst she was downstairs doing her daily chores. Grace was at school, so I'd get all the jewels to myself. I'd sometimes sneak a piece into my bed with me to keep me company in my fake illness. It became second nature to me to try and stay at home with her. It was always so good when it was just the two of us. I felt safe and secure. She didn't think I was naughty. I guess I must have tried to do it once too often because pretty soon they caught onto what I was doing and Dad told me that if I kept feeling ill like this I would have to go to the Doctor.

Our Doctor, Doctor O'Leary was lovely. When we had to go and see him with something Mum would say 'Deary, deary, Doctor O'Leary!' I didn't want to see him then though. He would know I was lying. I wondered could Doctors tell if you were naughty. I made a conscious effort from then on to be bright eyed and bushy tailed in the morning so I didn't have to go to see him. Mum had taken me to the Doctors once before as a child because I was always covered in bruises, all self-inflicted or from Granddad. I'd been scared stiff that he'd know my secret because Doctor's seemed to know everything. He'd just ruffled my hair and told Mum not to worry, that I was fine.

Back at Nana's house my adventures took a more down to earth turn. Whilst my face was pushed into the sofa as he took his satisfaction breathing heavier and heavier I would be walking hand in hand with imaginary friend at Marple Locks.

Marple Locks was a place we always went to as kids. It had a huge viaduct which Dad had told us was bottomless. We walked along there looking for animals, watching the birds, peering into the deep dark waters. Anything that took me away from the pain I felt if I stayed in the room, the stickiness that his pushing and panting created inside me. Anything to stop me being able to feel his penis in my hand or on my face. If the window was there I was ok.

After he'd finished I'd come back round slowly into my body. The pain gradually increasing as I became accustomed to being physical again.

The cracks on the windowsill grew deeper, just like my skin with the imprint of the pattern of their sofa on my cheek from where he had been pushing at me as he whispered his threats. All their windowsills were cracked, not like our shiny ones at home. They had bobbles of paint and cat hairs inside the stained paint like veins running through the house, their patterns forever ingrained in my head.

Their sofa was brown velvet, fringed with a really soft cotton-like thread and it had a pattern on one side and was plain on the other. Whenever Nana fancied a change she would swap the cushions round. I liked the plain side best because it left no marks on my skin. I hated the imprint, it made me feel dirty. It took what seemed like forever for the pattern to fade off of my skin and I could feel it for hours afterwards, for longer than I felt the pain or his stickiness inside me. Even when Nana and Grace got back from Aunty Jo's house I felt sure she would be able to see it on my face, surely she could? If not could she see my guilt?

I always hid my knickers afterwards, as if hiding them or throwing them away somehow got rid of the unseemliness from my body.

I hid them in the pocket of my jeans until I could get out into the back garden and throw them into the black bin that looked like a huge bucket with a lid and always smelt of last night's tea. I noticed that the blood wasn't coming as thick and fast as it used to by now. My body was relaxing as he did what he needs to do whilst breathing his drunken breath over my frail body. I had begun to relax more. What was better was that I had started to hold my food in for longer now. I would concentrate on keeping it in my stomach, not letting it pass too far into my bottom because if I didn't then he couldn't get as far into me and it didn't hurt as much. The feeling of relief when I knew that it was finished and I could go to the toilet and get rid of everything left inside me was incredible. It made the stickiness go quicker.

My feet still couldn't touch the floor properly yet if I sat on the toilet so I used to lean slightly off the seat so I could touch the floor so as it didn't hurt so much. I'd try to save up going to the toilet until I knew Mum and Dad were coming for me. It was the one act of defiance I had left in me. I was a naughty girl anyway so what did it matter!

That particular day after Nana got back from Aunty Jo's we went to the Legion. Granddad gone, Gramps bought us fizzy Vimto in a bottle and Salt and Vinegar crisps. The crisps in the Legion were always Bensons and came in greasy plastic packets but they tasted fantastic with the Vimto. I used to cram as many in my mouth at a time as I could crushing them against the roof of my mouth and taking a huge slurp of my fizzy drink at the same time feeling the liquid make them go all soggy.

Mike and his brother were there and Gramps set about his change back to his dark side by getting absolutely hammered. They were talking quietly together in the corner whilst I was playing with Grace cramming crisps into my mouth like I had been starved.

Mike looked over at me and smiled. I'd always felt like I was his favourite. Nobody else had favourites that I knew of between Grace and me, however he'd always told me he loved my giggle best. He had been watching me cram my crisps into my mouth and he came over and leant down. 'You're a naughty girl aren't you' he said. I froze, panic gripping me. 'Hey popsy', he said 'I'm only kidding. Come on Rachy, I'm sorry. I didn't mean to upset you'. I didn't want to be his girlfriend anymore. He knew. That's what they had been talking about, except of course it wasn't, but in my head it was. I couldn't look at him. Tears filled my eyes, big heavy tears that rolled down my cheeks. Granddad giggled his dirty laugh. 'Don't mind her Mike, she's a softy our Rachy!'. I never looked at Mike the same again. Mike bought me some more crisps and looked at me with puzzled eyes. He had the same kind of eyes as my imaginary friend. He looked at me sadly too. I'd done it again. I'd made someone I loved being with have sad eyes. Why did I do this? What was wrong with me? Perhaps he wanted me for his penis now? Perhaps that's why he bought me more crisps. I went into the toilet and sat on the cold seat wiping away my tears with the horrible scratchy toilet paper.

There was still a stain in my pants from where Granddad had been earlier so I stuffed paper inside them so it wouldn't touch my skin. 'I must throw them in the bin later before Mum and Dad come' I had thought to myself. When I came out of the toilet Mike had gone home and Granddad was slumped in the corner talking to yet more friends. I knew Mum and Dad would have been coming to get us soon and more than anything I wanted to be with my Dad. I wanted his safe secure smell, his arms around me, his clean laugh and the way he made me feel special in the nice sense, not the nasty way like Granddad.

That night when I got to the window my friend wasn't inside. He didn't open the window for me to get out and come play with him. He didn't want to go and sit in our tree house and he didn't want to walk through the fields. He just stared at me with sad eyes from beneath the oak tree. My eyes pleaded with him like they had pleaded with Granddad not to hurt me like this but he couldn't tonight. He was too sad for me. He didn't want to dream, he didn't want to pretend. He knew the reality and for once he was sad with me. I stared at him for hours and we stood either side of the window with tears streaming down our faces. But I didn't speak and neither did he. Maybe we just needed to cry.

My body lay cold in bed whilst I sat on the window and stared at my friend standing outside. I was cold because he was cold. When I got back into my body in bed to try to get warm I couldn't. No matter how much I pulled the duvet around me and tucked my feet in I just couldn't stop shaking. I knew Mum and Dad had been in bed for a while now so I wouldn't disturb them. I didn't want to wait for the sun to come up. I needed to be warm now. I crept out of bed onto the landing. I didn't want to get in with Mum and Dad that night. I didn't want to take the risk that they'd put me back in bed on my own. The airing cupboard was just outside my bedroom door. The sound of the water bubbling was familiar to me, the big red jacketed tank looked inviting and cosy. I climbed onto the first wooden shelf that the tank rested on to get close to the warmth. There was a shelf at the top also that had all the towels on, our bathroom towels and the warm beach towels we took on holiday with us.

Our bathroom towels were brown and beige. I loved them because they always smelt of home. They were dark brown with a swirling pattern on one side and reversed with beige on the other side. I buried my face into them, their softness surrounding me. I could get warm here. They would keep me safe. I climbed further into the airing cupboard, Pinky snuggled into my side. I reversed my body and backed onto the top shelf amongst the towels. The wood was warm against my skin and I could see everything on the landing from here. It was like my tree house. The heat was starting to flood into my bones now and for the first time that night I felt toasty. The landing light was bright and everything smelt so clean and fresh. Not like me. I wasn't clean and fresh anymore.

I stayed in there for hours just drinking in the smells and sounds of my home, feeling secure and safe. I eventually climbed down when the heating clicked on, before the sun came up and got back into my bed. I'd found my secret place, my own little den at home, no one could get to me there.

Chapter 6

The Move

Shortly after I was seven came the most exciting news of my life. We were moving house. Dad's job in the bank was taking him to the Isle of Man. I didn't even know where it was but it sounded interesting. Dad told us it was in the middle of the Irish Sea. I remember having visions of it being like a treasure island with coconut trees and monkeys and everyone would have really long beards and eat fresh fish from the sea. I loved fish.

I was sad to be leaving my friends, but the excitement of moving soon took over. Dad had to travel a lot to the island before we moved over and Mum missed him a lot. She used to cry at night because she missed him so much whilst he was away. I would hear her from my bed and long to go and cuddle her, but I never did.

All children have overactive imaginations, me being no exception and I used to believe that sharks or snakes were underneath the bed and if I stepped out that I would fall into the darkest pit full of them. I sometimes became scared that if I put any amount of flesh out of bed they would be able to pull me down into their world of darkness.

Dad was living in a hotel called the Palace Hotel. He brought us pictures of the front at Douglas and it seemed to be the grandest Hotel in the world. Before I saw it I imagined it would be like the Queens house because it was called the Palace and that it would have beautiful long pink flags blowing in the sea breeze from the turrets, because every palace had turrets. It was based slap bang in the middle of the promenade. I recall being quite disappointed when I first saw a picture of it because it wasn't like a palace at all, it was an imposing grey square building. There were no roses growing up the side as I had thought. There was no tower I could play with my imaginary friend in. But there was a pretty view of the whole of Douglas Bay. There were horse drawn trams that went along the front and a wide promenade with a high sea wall. The stones on the prom were made into patterns and there were bright flowers in beautifully maintained little gardens all the way along the side in between the prom and the road. The tram line ran down the middle of the road and there were occasional shelters in little walled gardens with massive green shiny benches in. The hotels were all painted, bright blues and greens, contrasting next to each other and they all had strange, foreign names. At the far end of the promenade there was a huge building called 'Summerland', which Dad had told us was the leisure centre. The whole thing looked so romantic.

Dad had put us in touch with two girls on the Island, that we had written to before moving over, and they had sent us some books about Manx cats. Manx cats have no tails although there are so many different folklores as to why that I never really found out the truth.

I loved the idea of living on an Island even if it wasn't the coconut Island I'd dreamt of. I didn't care for the name much because I didn't like the word man. I didn't like the shape of the land either, it looked the same as a man's back as he leant over and at the bottom there was the bit that stuck out, the penis, which was called the Calf of Man. I hated the penis although when I actually went to the Calf it became one of my favourite places to go because it was full of sea birds.

The day that we were moving was rapidly approaching. Nana was devastated we were going. Mum was the only child she had left in this country and now we were leaving too. Nana and Gramps wanted to spend more time with us before we left and we quite often went to stay the weekend with them, sometimes together, sometimes individually. It meant Mum and Dad got to spend some time on their own with each other because, of course, Dad was away all week. Occasionally Mum would let us come to the airport to pick him up and I would watch to see his familiar stride through the airport doors, envelope myself in his smell and pray that this was a weekend we could spend at home with them instead of going to Nana's.

We went over to Nana's for the day a few times before we left. The last time Gramps looked sad, he had sat in the living room looking into his glass and I'd sat at the kitchen table and had drawn a picture of him. I drew him in a bright yellow shirt, almost like a cowboy shirt. He had flared pants on and they were two tone, just like his pyjamas. His glasses I did in black, firm black rims. His face was perfect, if not a little large in comparison to his body. In between his legs was a bulge where his penis was, but it was covered so it was ok. I'd never drawn anything so well before. My pictures had been dark for a while until Mrs Wardell had made a comment to me about using bright colours because they were prettier. I always used the brighter colours after that. I was keen to please and be a good girl.

In his right hand I'd drawn a brandy glass filled with a dark brown liquid. It was so real I could almost smell it! I stuck the picture onto a piece of bright pink coloured paper and wrote 'My Gramps' at the bottom. The look on his face when I gave it to him was a picture. It is my favourite memory of him. He insisted on showing it to all his friends and they all loved it and told me how clever I was. I felt ten feet tall. I was the good girl he talked about. I'd done it! I'd pleased him without the penis! Mum and Dad loved it too, they chuckled, almost sadly, at the uncanny likeness and in particular the drink in the hand.

Moving day arrived sooner than we could prepare for and I was so excited. Mum was so sad to leave the house, but I got a day off school. Jenny, one of the girls that lived on the close we grew up in, said she would organise for all the children in the playground to shout goodbye at a certain time so we could hear it. I forgot completely and lied to her about hearing it because she'd obviously gone to so much trouble.

I looked around my room for the last time, said goodbye to the windows, said goodbye to my airing cupboard, where I had crept many a night to get warm. I waved at the old oak tree in the back garden and the acorns that would be falling in the autumn. As I looked through that window for the last time my imaginary friend appeared. I had been worried about him because I wasn't sure if he would come, but he had his bags and he was ready to go. All the smells of my family had gone and the house now smelt strange, empty, alone.

I stood underneath the blossom tree looking back towards the empty house. Mum was standing in the window with tears in her eyes. The close was filled with memories, my memories, putting on plays with my friends for our parents, the first time I'd ridden my bike, white knuckles clinging to the handlebars shouting Dad asking if he was still holding on. He shouted from the other end of the close that he was, it never occurring to me that he was so far away. Even the wall that I'd hit, the first time I seriously fell off my bike and got the new chippings from the road stuck in my forehead, seemed to be sad, like it was losing a friend. The grid outside the house, that I had spent hours rolling stones into, would no longer be the place I went to hear that wonderful plunking noise as they fell in.

As we climbed into Dad's car, Sukey in between Grace and me in her plastic carry box, I shed a tear, just one, for the tree house I would no longer be near, for the childhood I was leaving behind, and I looked forward to the future because on the Island I knew I would be safe.

The drive to Liverpool was filled with excitement because we were going on the boat for the first time. 'The Lady of Man' seemed like an enormous floating entertainment centre to me. There was a cinema down in the bowels of the ship and a lovely big black shiny chimney on the top with the Three Legs of Man painted on. Grace and I stood at the back of the ship worrying about Sukey stuck down below in the car section howling herself hoarse. We watched the Liver buildings disappear from sight, and then eventually England. We stayed there for ages with Mum and Dad sitting just a short distance away. Mum's eyes were red raw with all the tears she had shed during the day. Grace had been crying so she looked sad but I felt mixed. I knew nothing would change to me. It just worried me the unfamiliarity of it all. But, for the first time in my memory, I would be safe.

When the Isle of Man appeared on the horizon I could see the hotels on the front growing bigger and bigger. We were invited onto the captain's deck to see what the men sailing the ship did. The captain was a customer of Dad's and he seemed in full control watching all these people work to get the boat to go in the right direction. He was also a perfect look-a-like of Captain Birds Eye - with a great big long white beard. He asked me to pull this little cord hanging down. As I pulled it the ship let out its mighty fog horn. My God I'd never heard anything so loud and I'd made that noise. I thought they must have been able to hear that back at home. Only that wasn't going to be home anymore. This was going to be my new home.

We checked into the Palace Hotel as the house that we had bought wasn't ready yet. The staff must have got to know Dad well because they had left a basket of fruit, some flowers and I think, a bottle of champagne for Mum. We had an adjoining room to theirs connected by an internal door. There was a mini bar in the room, which of course I'd never seen before, and the bedding was beige and made up of mounds of blankets just like at Nana's. After dinner Grace and I unpacked some of our belongings and got into bed. It had been a really long day full of new things, which being ten and seven, were hard to take in.

After we had turned the lights out and Mum and Dad had pulled the door to from their room we whispered to each other in the semi-darkness. We both snuck out of bed to look outside at the sea rolling in quietly on the bay. On the headland there was an amusement park called White City and we sat watching the lights flicker on and off. They went off letter at a time and then flashed all together. It seemed so exciting. Dad had promised he would take us there soon.

The following day we were up early and ready to explore. Grace wanted to take Dad's binoculars down to the sea front to see if we could see home with them. This story is a bit of a legend in our family. All the boyfriends Grace and I had ever had have tired of hearing it from us!

We had crossed over the road and walked down onto the beach. The sand was damp so it stuck to our shoes and there were some very tiny circular twist shells dotted at regular intervals.

Mum and Dad were watching from the window. We waved at them, Grace holding Dad's new binoculars in her hands, I was too young to hold them.

Mum said to Dad 'Oh they're on the beach. Now they're going towards the sea. They're climbing on some rocks. Whoops Grace's fallen'. The rocks we had been climbing on were covered in seaweed and Grace had gone absolutely flying. We looked down at the binoculars - they were broken. We were going to get in so much trouble. These binoculars were Dad's pride and joy. We huddled around them looking to see if we could fix them, unbeknown to us that Mum and Dad could obviously tell they were broken from the way we were examining them, and they were in hysterics. We decided on the way back up to the hotel that I would go in first and explain and then Grace would come a few seconds later with the binoculars.

I knocked hesitantly on the door, Dad answered. 'There's been a bit of an accident' I said as Grace followed me sobbing her heart out. It was all too much for Mum who was literally rolling laughing. Dad swept us both up into his arms, as he always did, and said 'Are you alright', to which we both nodded. 'Well if you're alright that's all that counts'. Dad could do that. He could change a situation from feeling the most desolate thing in the world to just feeling plain old safe in a matter of seconds.

Shortly after that we moved into our new house in Saddlestone Valley, Braddan and started at the local primary school. The house was fantastic. It was half way up a really steep hill on the right hand side. Behind the house was a massive Copse, full of magnificent trees and all manner of ferns, grasses and wild flowers. The house very quickly smelt like ours because all of our things were there for us. It was and still is the favourite house I have ever lived in. I was so happy there. Grace and I had the upstairs to ourselves. As you walked around to the entrance of the house, which was at the side, there was a massive glass porch which was always warm inside. The front door was made of glass also and had a really squeaky handle on it. As you went in through the front door the ceiling was double height and there was a fabulous open staircase with metal railings all the way up. We used to play "daft bats" on those railings which involved hooking your legs over the top and dangling over the hallway below upside down. But the best thing about that house was that we had locks on our bedroom door.

The Living room come Dining room was an L shaped area with a beautiful big marble fireplace that Mum and Dad had had installed. The white outside encased the shiny marble which was brown patterned on a cream background. Part of the marble swirl looked exactly like Bugs Bunny which Grace and I always loved, and the fire was an electric one with bars encasing hot bars and a light underneath glass shards that was supposed to make it look like a real fire but never really had the desired effect.

Out of the front window you could see the whole of Saddlestone Valley right across up to Ballakameen High School at the very top of the hill on the other side. Our primary school was right down in the bottom of the valley and had a tunnel of trees leading up to it. It was right next to a graveyard full of hundreds and hundreds of decrepit old stones from the 1800's. I was both fascinated by and terrified of this graveyard, with its huge stone wall encompassing the front leading right up to our school.

The headmaster at the school was a lovely skinny man with a bald head, red nose but a big belly at the front. He always wore a tweed suit with a tank top underneath and soft brown leather shoes. He introduced us in Assembly the first morning we arrived and explained where we had come from. I was in the top infants which meant I exited the hall from assembly to the left whereas Grace was Top Juniors so she went right. I couldn't wait to see her at first break, just so I could see somebody familiar. I was very keen to show the teacher how clever I thought I was and made sure I did my best joined up writing for her that first day. She was impressed because they hadn't learnt joint up yet. She told me that maybe I should try to learn with the rest of the class so I didn't feel left out. I sat with a girl called Karen (pronounced the manx way Care-ann) who had beautiful Ginger hair and a girl, Greeba with thick dark brown plaits and blue national health glasses. They made me feel really welcome.

I settled into school really quickly as did Grace, I think it was probably a good age for us to have moved because we were very adaptable. I would quite often see my imaginary friend loping up to the top of the field just keeping a watchful eye over me as I played in the playground. The only thing that disappointed me about the school was that you couldn't eat crisps for your snack at break. I had been used to taking whatever I wanted out of my lunchbox and got done for eating a packet of Prawn Cocktail Wickets. I was sorely disappointed. I didn't know you had to eat fruit instead. Apart from that the school seemed ok to me.

We developed a lot of friends in the neighbourhood and at the weekends Mum and Dad rarely saw us. There was a path that ran just beyond the back of the fence at the bottom of our garden. In the fence there was a small hole just big enough to fit through. It was all black around the edges like it had been burnt at some point and Mum used to go mad with us for getting these difficult to get out stains out until eventually they cottoned onto what we were doing and we were told very firmly not to do it again. Grace and I would use this entrance to sneak in and out of at home all the time. At the very top of the road there was a large circular turning with a small path at the end. The path ran in between two houses identical to ours, only their eves were painted green to the left and red to the right, not like ours which were turquoise. If you walked up that path it led to a huge field where we spent hours building dens, riding our bikes, playing hide and seek with our friends and generally larking about.

We had met loads of people when we started going to school and subsequently church. The church in Braddan is famous for being on one of the worst bends on the TT race course. It's a dog leg bend, absolutely lethal. We saw many an accident on that road when the TT races were on.

At Sunday School I started to believe in God again of a sort. We used to mess about for the majority of the session then at the end we would be taught something from the bible and say our prayers. I suppose I had begun to believe again because my life had taken a turn for the better. We had so much freedom here. Looking back now it's because there was no crime at all in the area. It seemed to be twenty years behind England in its lifestyle. We could go out and play for hours on end and Mum just didn't have to worry. Perhaps there was a God because he'd taken me away from being special. Here I was normal.

Shortly after we moved in Mum broke her toe. As happy as Grace and I were here Mum became really miserable and unhappy. She missed her friends from back home, she missed her family, she missed Bramhall. So she decided to further her education again by joining the local college.

Dad had just bought his new car, a bright blue ford cortina with letters spelling out MAN U in the reg. The other car, a blue Chevette had the same. God I thought we were posh having the number plates so like a football club. Dad had chosen those two sets of numbers after Bryan Robson and Bryan McClair who played at six and seven at the time. The blue Chevette had a fake leather interior and in the back seat there was a small hole which if you slid your finger into you could feel the springs of the chair. But that didn't matter to me. I always felt chauffeur driven with our private plate! Mum got to have the Chevette all the time as opposed to the clapped out mini she had driven when we lived in England. She subsequently got a shiny red Volvo 340 which I loved although the plate was just plain old Manx one which would never be as cool as the previous one.

The driveway at the front of the house was big enough for both cars to fit on and we had a massive double garage that the cars went into leaving Grace and I loads of space to play at the front. I had a shiny brown bike called an 'Amber' which I adored and Grace's was blue with pink writing on. We rode our bikes up to the top of the hill every day screeching half way down to where we had to stop at our house because the hill became too steep.

The best thing about the house though was the size of the airing cupboard. It had two large double doors and so much space that I could get in for hours on end. We would often hide in there amongst the familiar smells of washing powder and the wooden slats that held up the three sets of shelves.

Our bedrooms were massive and had big wooden door frames with patterned glass in which meant we could have the doors shut at night if we wanted to and still have loads of light in the room. I made pictures out of the patterns on the door, one of Kermit the frog and one that said love. I loved those doors because you could see who was outside. My imaginary friend and I felt safe here. We could fly out of the window into the Copse, over the whole of Saddlestone Valley, down past the Quarterbridge Pub to the main road and eventually down to Douglas. We flew along the beach laughing at the waves, marvelling at the trams that were driven by huge horses. We visited Summerland and White City, we skated along the prom together, we ran in the waves. I didn't need him as much now but he was always there, just watching and waiting, in case I did.

The summer holidays passed in a blur of excitement. They had taken forever to pass in England but on the Island there was always something to do. Quite often we would be allowed to take the train up to Port Erin with our friends. There must have been about twenty kids all hanging out of the old-fashioned steam train windows trying to catch the wild flowers that grew up the sides of the train track as we chugged by. Or we went to the Lido arcade on the front at Douglas that had a huge soft play area for kids upstairs. Or we skated down the prom with Dad, him catapulting us forward when he got tired of running along with us. There was always a place to visit, Castles, beaches, the mountain where legend has it on a clear day you can see six kingdoms, England, Ireland, Scotland, Wales, the kingdom of Man and the kingdom of God, the Laxey Wheel and what seemed like thousands of glens made up of natural flowers and babbling streams where we could paddle.

I went into the juniors at school that September. I remember feeling so grown up then. My life couldn't have been more perfect. I'd almost managed to forget that I was supposed to be a naughty girl. I'd put my memories into a place in my head where I didn't have to think about them. It wasn't important to me any more, I was safe and sound with my family. Nobody could take me away.

The first time I remember Nana visiting was the first summer we were there. Mum had broken her toe and she was feeling really down in the dumps. She hadn't settled in properly and she wanted Nana to come over. Nana loved the Island and everything about it. She always saw the romance in things, just like me.

We took her to all of our favorite places, to meet all our new friends. I enveloped myself in her warmth and love without there being any kind of threat for the first time I could think of. However, at night the same old dreams returned to haunt me I think triggered of by that smell of talc. His presence was everywhere in my house and I hated it.

We took Nana over to Peel beach. I loved it there because there was a café called the Rollercoaster Café where we always bought ice cream and fizzy drinks. They sold the same kind of cheap crisps that the Legion had sold. Inside the café was a jukebox which if Grace and I had spare money we would play different songs from. The Kids from Fame were all the rage and Grace thought it was hilarious because I thought the song High Fidelity was actually Hi Penelope. She took the mick out of me for years about that. The building that the café was in was painted pink and the sign that said the name was a tall and vertical with the letters one on top of the other. Anyway so there we were sitting on the beach in a line, me, Mum, Dad, Grace and then Nana and this dog came over to be friendly. It sniffed me, then Mum, Dad, Grace and when it got to Nana it sniffed, cocked its leg and peed right on her back. We started giggling, Nana was almost hysterical, she was laughing that much that she rolled off down the beach. We were crying with laughter! From that day on I always swore Nana smelt of talc and dog pee!

Time came for her to go home and things settled down again for a while. We occasionally used to speak to them on the phone but nothing serious. That is until he came to visit.

As I watched Gramps getting off the plane I shrank back further and further into my Dad as I knew that each step he took nearer to us was a step closer to pain for me. For the first few days he was Gramps, just plain old Gramps and I loved it. We showed him all the places we had shown Nana. He wanted to buy a hat, 'a nat' as he pronounced it from the port near to Douglas bay. There were a row of little shops along the side that sold everything that a fisherman would require and he loved it down there. Because Dad was with me all the time I felt safe. At night Grace and I were sleeping in the same room again so I knew that would be ok. He was sleeping in my bed though. My clean bed was dirty now. Dirty with his leathery skin, his brown pyjamas and his penis.

On the Saturday night Grace had arranged to go and stay at a friend of hers, Susie. Susie was a really pretty girl with long dark hair. He parents owned a French restaurant in Douglas which I thought was so exciting. We had been there to eat on several occasions when Dad had something important to celebrate. Or sometimes even when he wanted to treat Mum to a meal out with some of their friends they would go there for a slap up dinner. I loved the smell of the restaurant. It smelt exotic and they had red and white check table cloths with a white one over the top like a diamond, and candles in the middle of the tables mounted into empty French wine bottles. It was so romantic. However tonight I couldn't think about the restaurant. Tonight I knew I was in danger. He had been drinking wine at tea time and I knew wine meant Granddad would be on his way.

I didn't sleep at all. I heard my bed squeak quietly as he crept towards my bedroom door. I heard him tip toe across the landing and I was mad at myself. Why hadn't I locked the door? I had known this would happen. Why hadn't I done it sooner?

As he slid his hands into my knickers probing and feeling his way back to his naughty girl he had his penis in his hand. But I wasn't there. I was far away with my imaginary friend. He had taken me to be with Grace and Susie in their restaurant, where the smells were clean and fresh not of alcohol and darkness. My throat filled with bile as he pressed his prickly moustache to my lips. The landing light was bright shining into the room and I know he saw the fear in my eyes. I willed the tears back as much as I could. I didn't want to give him the satisfaction of seeing me cry. He whispered his threats all the while touching my chest, asking me if I'd missed him and did I want him. And of course I let him like the dutiful idiot I had become.

In the morning I hurt like hell all over. It had been so long that my body wasn't accustomed to accommodating him. As we waved him off at the airport I cried. Mum and Dad thought it was because I'd missed him, but I knew it was because my bed had had him in it, Grace's bed was soiled, dirty, evil. I wanted to burn them both. I wanted to burn myself to get his smell, taste, texture off of my skin. But I couldn't reach the matches in the kitchen, so I was trapped in my tainted skin, skin that was becoming more and more like his. I tanned really easily and when I did I could see that mine had the same make-up as his and I hated it. I wanted to rip it off piece by piece. How could I though? How could I? They would know? The further his plane got away, the quieter I became. I didn't even want to say Hello to the fairies on the Fairy Bridge, although Dad said I had to because he had heard so many stories about people not saying Hello and then their car breaking down 100 yards down the road. The Isle of Man was full of folklore like that, magical but sometimes scary for a child.

Gramps stayed again whilst we were there but he never came to me at night. He touched me during the day when we were alone, sometimes even when Mum and Dad were near, curling his hands around my chin, making me tough his penis inside his trousers, pressing his hairy face onto mine. To this day I hate moustaches on a man. But most of the time he was just Gramps. I had my victory that time. I used to wait until Dad had tucked me in and then Mum would check on me last thing before they went to bed and then I would sneak out of bed and lock the door. I felt safe when the door was locked. He tried it once but he couldn't do it. I laughed silently under my cover. It was his last night, he wouldn't be coming again. I had found my escape.

I hated going back into my own room after he'd gone. The room smelt of him and it took me ages to settle back into a normal routine.

We went home every Christmas to visit them and stay with Dad's family, but I never remember anything happening at Christmas. Christmas was my safe time. Perhaps he wanted to make sure I got presents from Father Christmas?

The Christmas I was nine Grace took me by the hand and led me to the cupboard at the top of the stairs at our Aunty's house. Their house was a bungalow that had had a loft conversion. The stairs were opposite the front door down the hall and they were super. They were open stairs and Grace and I used to play "daft bats" there too, which involved us sticking our legs through each stair and hanging upside down. It had been a really traumatic day for me because whilst playing daft bats I had decided that I'd try and stick my head through instead of my legs. Of course I got stuck there, legs dangling beneath me screaming my head off. Dad supported my weight underneath whilst Mum shoved Strawberry flavoured Chewits into my mouth to stop me crying, they eventually pulled me out by brute force. I didn't do that again in a hurry.

Anyway Grace took me by the hand to the little under eaves cupboard at the top of the stairs and threw it open to reveal all of the presents inside. I was devastated, not as devastated as the rest of the family though. I am youngest in my generation and they wanted me to believe for as long as I possibly could, for their sakes really more than mine.

Uncle Andrew dressed up as Father Christmas to try and convince me and I went along with it for their sakes, but I knew now. It didn't matter if I was a good girl for Father Christmas, as long as Mum and Dad never found out I would still get presents. This year was the first year I had been given money to buy my own presents – I'd always known that we bought our friends presents, they didn't come from Santa – and I was so excited to be mature enough to get my own things. I had a whole ten pounds to spend on everyone. I had been in Douglas and gone to this beautiful trinket shop that sold souvenirs to tourists and beautiful pieces of glass from the glass factory near Tynwald and bought Mum an ornament of a Sheepdog which I adored and I couldn't wait to see her face. I had spent £4.99 on this ornament because Mum was precious to me and everyone else's presents were probably rubbish but I couldn't wait to see her face because she'd know how much it had been and she'd know how much I loved her. It was the best present ever and of course she loved it. So although the Christmas magic had gone in someway it had been reborn for me in the giving of my Christmas presents. All my happiest memories are of Christmas.

Chapter 7

The Return

By this point in my life I was in the Juniors at Primary School and had a teacher I adored called Mr James. Mr James always reeked of Kouros aftershave and seemed really cool. He was single much to the delight of the Mums. He loved everything to do with nature and I spent the happiest year of my school life in his class making nature trails, learning about birds and butterflies. All the Mums fancied Mr James and got more 'dolled up' when they knew he would be around at the end of the day. He was the first teacher I ever had a crush on. When the time came to leave him I didn't want to but like most things in my life all good things come to an end, just like my safety on the Island had. Moving up into the next class was going to be hard because they couldn't accommodate all the children in my year so the brightest were going to skip a class into the year above for two years as opposed to one with Mr Veron, the head teacher. I was picked! I was so proud of myself as were Mum and Dad. There were eight of us picked to go up, into the biggest classroom in the school with the best library. It was a fantastic classroom with beautiful big wooden hinge topped desks inscribed with what seemed to me like a billion past students names. Grace had been in this class before me and I had thought she was so grown up.

I ran for student president of the school that year and came third which sounds really good until you hear there was only four in the race! The boy that won it, Julian's Dad was a local politician had loads of laminated flyers printed. All I had was my speeches that Mum and Dad had helped me with. Julian had bought cookies for everyone on the day of the vote. I was gutted! I got my picture in the paper though. There I was smiling wearing my best jumper from Benetton, my favourite shop. Julian wore a shirt, tie and v-neck sweater for the results. I had felt positively scruffy. My ideas for improvement in the school had been quite good. I'd given nine speeches on the things that I felt could have used change in the school which Mum and Dad had helped me with and written out for me and detailed how I would go about implementing my ideas. My speeches were logical, not bravado from the mouth of a local politician, like Julian's. I hated him, he was so smug! He'd also got his younger sister to get all her friends to vote for him. Grace had already left the school so I couldn't bank on her friends votes. I cried into my imaginary friends shoulder that night. I had been right all along. I didn't fit in! I wasn't good enough. Jonathan, the boy that came last had taken it really well, although in my eyes he couldn't have been as serious about it as I was. I could have made a difference. It would have been my time to make myself a good girl. For my consolation prize I was allowed to be milk monitor for a term which was almost unheard of from a middle infant student. I loved the feeling of giving everyone their milk and collecting the shiny coppers from each of my classmates.

Shortly after Christmas Dad decided it was time to redecorate our bedrooms. Grace and I had swapped rooms prior to that so I was now in the back again as I had been when we first moved here. I loved the back room. It was the biggest room in the house apart from the living room. My favourite bit, the under eaves were all plastered so you could play in there unlike the eaves in the front room which had asbestos insulation through-out and Mum and Dad used them for storage of the things we needed to keep but didn't use often enough to have out all the time. Grace and her friends had written all over the inside of the back room eaves filling it with of graffiti about who they thought was 100% fit as we used to say.

The day Dad took us to choose the wall paper Grace went for a fairly simple pattern, however I chose one with a thousand spots in all different pastel colours. I adored it although Dad was worried it would give me a headache looking at it. That was the least of his worries really. Just after he had finished decorating it he and Mum came in to sit with me. They had already been in to see Grace so I knew it was something serious. Perhaps they knew and they had been telling Grace I would be leaving soon. Dad picked me up into his arms whilst Mum sat on the bed and they explained that they had something to tell me. 'Oh no this was bad' I thought. We were going back to England because Dad's job had moved again. I buried my mouth into Dad's shoulder as tears rolled silently down my cheeks, my eyes peeping over the top of his shoulder looking at my Mum. My shiny, new, clean, spotty bedroom still smelt of damp wallpaper paste, not of memories past, and now I had to leave it. The first clean thing I'd had and now I had to go back to that place, that place that was even more unsafe. I didn't want to go. I didn't want to leave the Island where I had been happy most of the time. I didn't want to have to go and stay with Nana and Granddad at weekends again, or leave my friends, or my school, but more importantly I didn't want to leave the lock on my bedroom door. I knew I wouldn't have one in the new house, I just knew it.

On their last visit, Uncle Daniel & Aunty Jill had given me a writing pad from Daniel's company in Canada. It was blue and it had the shadow of a large piece of machinery on it, with a shiny hard plastic cover on the outside. I'd loved this pad when they'd given it to me, however now it was the way I would tell my friends I was leaving them and I would forever hate it. I sat down under the new duvet cover to write letters to all my friends. I took them into school the next morning with my tears mixing with the shiny blue ink making some of my perfectly formed letters cloud with sadness. I didn't want to go and everyone knew it.

Mr Veron tried to make a special fuss of me because he could see I was unhappy. He even let me use the purple pen to do my work in school that day. We had to write a story about a journey to Nottingham, as we had been reading about Robin Hood, and he let me read mine out first. He made it a really cool thing that I would be taking the first step of the journey to Nottingham by taking the flight back to England and all my mates were jealous. Catriona, one of the girls in the class, was really good at creative writing and her story had the best start ever, it started with 'Feeling airsick again!'. She read her story directly after mine and I felt very inadequate. Not only was I unclean but stupid as well. My self-hatred had started to spiral out of control again and we weren't even leaving until the end of the school year.

Those few months were strange for me really because I was scared of getting comfortable. When we had moved to the Island I hadn't really been affected by losing my friends and I hadn't felt that much of a wrench. I had been coming to something better, to what I had believed would be a safer place. Now the dread weighed so heavy on my heart I felt sure the plane it was planned we should leave on wouldn't be able to take off with the extra weight.

As the day got nearer and nearer the strain was evident on Mum and Dad. After not wanting to come to live on the Island so badly, Mum had really settled here. She had done her Teacher Training qualification and finally had a career of her own and a fantastic social circle of friends. We were getting older now and needed her less and less as our independence grew. One of her close friends, a guy called James was fabulous! He had a wicked sense of humour and treated Grace and I like we were young ladies rather than kids which was always quite cool. Then there was Clare, who Mum had set up with one of Dad's friends, Hamish, and they were now getting married. Grace and I were going to be bridesmaids. I know there were hundreds of people who adored Mum at the college, but those were two were the main ones.

It wasn't just Mum though. Dad seemed to love everything about the Isle of Man and I just couldn't understand why he wanted us to leave. He explained more recently it was because the opportunities Grace and I would have had there would have been more limited than if we moved back to England and he wanted to move before Grace took her options for her O Levels.

Of course the day arrived when we were to pack everything up. Our cosy home stripped bare, all bar my beautiful spotty wallpaper in my room that would now belong to another little girl, packed into large removal crates. We left all the graffiti under the eaves, kind of our bit of history in the house. My toys were packed, my clothes, my bedding, everything clean and on its way to storage because we couldn't move into our new house for a few weeks. In any case we were going on holiday to Tenerife first and then had Clare and Hamish's wedding to go to in Liverpool. We were to be their bridesmaids and had the most wonderfully grown up peach dresses. I felt like a princess in mine and everybody who saw us told us we looked fantastic.

Dad was going to drive Mum, Grace and I to the airport and then fol-low us over on the boat with the car and the removal van. The previous Christmas when we had got the boat to England it had been a Gale Force Nine and Grace and I had been so ill Dad had said he would never take us on the boat again.

On my last day of school all my friends gathered around me as we took photographs and swapped addresses, even Mr James gave me a hug and a kiss. He said my part of the nature trail, which we had done in his class, would always be there in my name so no one could ever forget I had gone to that school. I thought that was such a lovely thing to say that I cried and he ruffled my hair and told me I'd be fine. I was the envy of a few Mums that day! Mr Veron said goodbye to me personally in assembly and my friends and I made up a dance to a song that was out in the charts called 'Bad Boys' which I think was by a band called Miami Sound Machine which we got to perform in front of the school. We all hugged and cried at the end of the performance because even though I had only been there three years it had felt like forever. He read out a poem I had written about Autumn days which had been on the wall for the last few months in a big collage of leaves and poetry, it was the only time I had a piece of writing up on the wall in the hall and I had been so proud.

As Mum drove me away from the school to the empty house I was inconsolable. Nothing would make me smile. I didn't want this new school with the stupid name. I didn't want to make new friends and have to try to fit in again, I wanted Braddan School where I knew each brick in the hand-built wall between the playground and the field. I wanted the sick bed where I was sent to lie down when I was ill. I wanted to be able to smell Mr James' aftershave at at least 100 paces, but most of all I wanted my friends to be there. I had some good friends, all of whom had made a real fuss of my leaving and sworn faithfully they would write. We'd sealed it with spit on our hands so it had to be true!

I cried all the way to the airport, especially as I said Goodbye instead of Hello to the fairies at the Fairy Bridge, big silent tears just rolling down my cheeks. Even when I got on the plane and was given a Barley Sugar sweet to stop my ears from hurting, my tears wouldn't stop.

The Manx Airlines Planes were all white with shiny green stripes and the three legs on man on the tail. Some of the fleet of planes was so small they could only seat 14 people. They were mainly propeller driven and you could feel the vibrations from underneath your seat no matter where you sat. Sometimes on the smaller planes the stewardess would come round with a flask of tea or coffee as opposed to the massive shiny tea pots on the larger planes I had been on in my life. The Stewardesses were really pretty and always had perfect make-up. On one of our frequent trips to and from the Island Alvin Stardust was on the plane. We had seen him at Manchester

Airport, Dad had walked past and said "Hello Alvin" to our wide eyed amazement. Alvin had smiled back warmly at Dad and said hello back. That had sealed it for me. My Dad knew everyone!

When we arrived back in England we dropped our bags at some friends' house, met Dad and turned straight back round for the airport, flying out to Tenerife. I suppose it was a great diversionary tactic on the part of Mum and Dad plus it also meant Dad got a break before moving into the new house and starting his new job with his family safely ensconced.

The holiday itself was fantastic! We made loads of new friends, probably a good thing for our confidence because we had left so many old friends behind. Grace and I both joined the kids clubs, me in the younger group and her, the older. There were structured activities every day and for each activity you won you got a certificate. When you had six certificates you got a Sol Hotel Gold Medal and I got one on our last day. Thinking about it they must have fixed the last pass the parcel so that I won so that I got the medal but I didn't care, I got my moment of glory when they played the Rocky music and I went up in front of all of the parents in the entertainments hall in the evening and was presented with my medal by Joanna the Entertainments Manager.

This holiday changed my life for a few reasons. One of them was a boy called Steven. He had dark hair with a big flick at the front that he must have spent hours perfecting in the mirror. He was really tanned and had gorgeous dimples. As usual he fancied Grace not me, nothing strange there then, she was the most beautiful teenager, so natural and refined with her wet look perm. He was sixteen, she was thirteen and they soon hooked up. They made the most gorgeous couple but soon split up because she had lied to him about her age. I became his sounding board. We talked for what felt like forever by the pool table about Grace and the boy I fancied Jonathan, who thought I was too young for him, which in all fairness I was. Steven's sisters were horrible to him. After Grace he had another holiday romance with a girl called Kirsten who was horrible and hated the fact that he spent so much time with me, a mere ten year old girl.

Steven was a gentleman to me! He never even kissed me. He held my hand as we talked but he never laid a finger on me. He talked to me about his past relationships and about how much he hated his parents, he told me how much he wished I was older so we could be a proper couple, but that's as far as he took it. I didn't really understand what he meant. What could be different about an older relationship than I had already done. I knew of course about sex and what that meant and that people did it all the time. Maybe his family didn't start until later was my initial thought and the only way I could rationalize what he was saying.

During the second week there was a Roman night where everyone had to dress up in togas, all makeshift from the sheets on the beds in the room. I'd insisted that I made my own as having the staff make them for me would mean taking my clothes off in front of the lads in the room and I wasn't about to do that. That night Steven took me for a walk by the pool. He held my hand as we sat by the water and told me his darkest secret then he asked me for mine. I nearly told him! I nearly did but something held me back. The friendship he had given me was something so pure and true that I didn't want to taint it with my dirty darkness. I wanted him to think of me as being pure, not naughty. I wrote to him for a few years after that holiday but never saw him again. I'd love to know where he is now just to tell him how grateful I was that he was so sweet to me. He was a dark haired version of my imaginary friend, the only man in my life who had ever come close to being similar, besides my Dad.

For the first time I had begun to question what was happening to me and whether it was in fact as common place as I believed, more than that whether it was right. It had never felt right, having such a big secret and had weighed heavy on my mind. Could it be wrong though for my Grand-dad to do these things? I just didn't know.

The second thing I recall about this particular holiday was a girl called Tracey that Grace became friendly with. Tracey was fifteen and she had the most enormous boobs.

A waiter from the restaurant had collared Tracey in one on toilets and tried to touch her, she had told her parents and they were furious and de-manded that the man concerned be sacked. Listening to Tracey and Grace talking about it was an eye opener and I lay awake until dawn thinking things over in my head. Could I be wrong? Did this not happen to every-one? Was it just me? I had to start a new school in a few weeks would this just be another reason that I wouldn't fit in. I really must have been dirty and naughty if this happened to me and no one else. The waiter had said that Tracey had egged him on to the management staff. Had I done that?

My confusion gained more and more momentum as the holiday went by and I felt increasingly alone as there was no one I could ask. The only one person I could ask was Granddad and I was too scared for that. These feelings of sheer isolation just further exasperated my self hatred and wish to hurt myself and I would frequently kick things or scratch myself if no one was looking out of sheer frustration.

With all this in my mind and the worry of the move I became very insular and moody particularly towards Grace. I had idolized her for so long but now I didn't know how to handle her. I wanted to talk to her but I couldn't. I became such a brat towards her that it's a wonder I got back off that holiday in one piece. I was beginning to grow quiet quickly and was catching Grace up in size so she couldn't beat me as often in fights anymore.

We returned to move into a local hotel in Lymm whilst we were waiting for the new house to be ready. There was a big Yew tree in the garden and I loved it, almost as much as the old Oak tree in Bramhall, for a different reason though. The Oak tree was a faithful friend whereas the Yew tree was something traditional to me, they always had them in a cemetery to ward off evil spirits. Maybe my evil spirits would be kept at bay here? Maybe I would be safe? It could be a new start for me too!

Dad had been traveling back and to for a while now. He had been staying in the Hotel whilst he had been getting to grips with his new job. He was more senior in the bank now and had been given a company car, a white Rover which was 'seriously cool' because it was the first car we had that had electric windows and as well as having the window controls on each door Dad had a master control panel in the front with him which he used to torment us with all the time.

I adored the new house, although I was a bit gutted that Grace got the best room, over the garage. My new bedroom had all my familiar things in it but it didn't feel like home yet.

Of course one of the first set of visitors was Nana and Gramps. They were delighted to have us back here in the country so close to them and started to arrange when they could see Grace and I. Grace didn't want to go, she was thirteen and got more of a say in what she did, but I was ten and didn't really get a choice. I had my plan though for when I had to go there. I was going to stick to Nana like glue. I wouldn't leave her side. If what was happening was the 'right thing' then he wouldn't be scared of hiding it from Nana, because I knew that marriages didn't have secrets.

The first visit went fine – he was Gramps, the smells were the same and I didn't stay over, Mum came for me. Perhaps I had imagined it all, perhaps it was all a bad dream? I questioned everything about my life and how I had come to this point. I think that visit lulled me into a false sense of security, made me wonder more if it was all in my head.

And if it wasn't in my head then I knew it was wrong, that it didn't happen to everybody, but I didn't know how to stop it. I felt so alone. The loneliness felt like a cancer eating me away inside, a blackness that no amount of medication could have ever cured or made better.

Chapter 8

School

The new school was on the other side of the village to our house. Mum dropped me at my school and Grace at the high school that day and left us to it. We were both delivered into our respective classes by the office staff. I was devastated to find out I would be in the class below Top Infants although I was a Top Infant because there were too many students. I'd gone from being the brightest to what looked like being the under achiever. I never really settled with my teacher. He used to criticize my writing and made me redo work I had covered the year before. I was going through a phase where each story I wrote ended up in someone disappearing or getting hurt. My frustration grew! I had always loved writing my stories and poetry as a form of expression, yet he seemed to want me to write nice happy dainty stories that "girls should write". He decided that I was too much of a dreamer and tried to convert me to writing about different things. Inside me was blackness, how could I write cheerful stories when all I could feel was black. I had become so adept at hiding my feelings and emotions.

Despite all my worry I fitted in fairly quickly, as did Grace. I made friends with a girl called Louisa and for the first time in my life had a 'best friend'. I'd never really felt comfortable having a best friend before and had always drifted from group to group of people. I was always too scared of getting settled in case he had told my parents and I'd have been taken away but now I knew that wasn't true even though I didn't know what to do about it. My loneliness grew, whereas before I thought everyone went through the same and kept it inside now I knew it was just me and that was scarier than anything.

I even managed to have a few boyfriends – one of whom was the first boy ever to kiss me properly. I didn't really enjoy it but had felt under pressure to do it as we were in the youth club and everyone was egging us on. I dumped him shortly after that. I couldn't handle being in a relationship where I felt pressure. I could cry at the drop of a hat and got badly picked on because of it. There were a few of the lads in my year at school that picked up on this so I learnt to cry internally. I would channel all my energy into staying angry on the outside where inside I would be dying. It didn't matter what anyone said to me I just let it wash over my head whilst secretly silently crying inside and then when I got to the toilet I could let go. I used to fake illnesses to get out of school all the time. I had reached an age where I knew that every illness didn't get you taken to the doctors. Besides I knew that the Doctor wouldn't be able to tell unless I told him. I got away with it for a while but my attendance record was terrible which was evident when my school report for that year came. I don't think Mum noticed but I did and it shocked me.

My time at primary went really fast and High School was looming quicker than I'd have liked. I'd only just settled into this one and was going to have to move again which was really intimidating. I knew there would be a whole new crowd to fit into and the thought of that terrified me.

My sense of security at Nana's became stronger. I felt as though what had happened was getting further and further away from the present. I'd become confident that it was over and even started to enjoy the time that I spent there with them. He had become the Gramps I loved again. He didn't drink as much except when he went to the Legion. Then I always stayed with Nana in sight and rarely slept over anymore but I felt at home, even dare I say it comfortable. Foolish really!

My eleventh birthday was on a Tuesday. I was staying over at Nana's the following Saturday. I'd never really gone in for my birthday much as I'd always associated it in the past with being in that house and the start of this whole mess. I was confident that everything would be fine.

I had even thought things would be fine as he moved across my bedroom floor to get to me again. And things weren't actually that bad because I got away. I hadn't been to the toilet and he didn't try to penetrate me. He just played mind games taunting me with his soft voice telling me things that he wanted from his 'special girl' whilst he held me like a Gramps, but all the while whisperings filthy disgusting things into the back of my head whilst I kept my bottom firmly clamped to the bed, to the clean covers that Nana and I had made the bed up with earlier that day. Except they weren't clean now. They were filled with his disgusting words. They were filled with his penis being in my hand and him rocking backwards and forward onto it until he came on me and wiped the stuff away. I felt it for hours again afterwards. Why was this happening to me? What had I done to deserve this? It wasn't fair! I didn't understand why he took so much pleasure out of making me feel so bad. I know he saw it when he looked in my eyes, I know he saw my fear and confusion. Maybe that's why he did drink? Maybe that's why he was so nice in Gramps mode, to overcompensate for this part of him. This horrible, evil dirty part that made me feel so desperately alone.

I felt safe nowhere now, not at home, not at school, not out with my friends and most certainly not here, not even when Nana was there now. I knew he could strike at any moment. Whether it was a kiss that he held for too long, or whether he touched my breasts, which were now developing from puppy fat into proper shapely, adolescent boobs, granted not big ones but boobs all the same.

At high school I had settled in on the outside very well. I had kind of moved on from Louisa and was now best friends with a girl called Looby. Looby was the prettiest girl in the class. She had long dark curly hair, beautiful brown eyes and I thought she was gorgeous. She and I were inseparable because on our first day at school we had been told to sit together. She had come from a private primary school so knew no-one and I had no friends from my old school in the class with me, except for a few boys, but I wasn't really interested in any of them because they were stupid! I had of course had a few boyfriends by now but I was petrified of one of them touching me because I knew how much it hurt and the feelings it created inside me.

My most serious boyfriend so far, Stuart, had dumped me because I wouldn't let me touch my boobs. The minute he tried I froze, I was so scared. He said I was a kid and that he wanted more being a lad of 13 and all. In fact that's something that I tease him for constantly now because we meet up once a year at the local carnival and have an all day drinking session as has become tradition. It's become a standing joke in our circle of friends.

So Looby and I became best friends. We went everywhere together, and eventually, had boyfriends who were friends too. We used to go into town together on a Saturday just walking around thinking we were really cool. We were both tall and therefore looked older and got quite a bit of attention from the lads. We didn't know how to handle it though. Looby was cool to me. She ate Big Macs and Mars Bars, something I'd never really done before and she wore really funky clothes that her Mum bought her. Her Mum was really funny.

We played netball together for the team and even our parents became friends, of a sorts, because they were always collecting or dropping off at one or others houses.

In the first year I had also become friendly with a girl called Jane who was in the third year. She seemed so confident and pretty and she was really popular. We started going to Athletics training together three times a week with a guy called Jay who was in her year. I became quite a fast runner although I wasn't as fast as her. Mum and Dad loved the fact that I was training so hard. I had always been against smoking and they thought that this would keep me away because I knew I needed all my lung power for the track. I became quite an accomplished athlete both track and field and was also becoming a strong swimmer. In my mind I knew I was training for the one day when I would be able to say no. I knew the day would come that I would be bigger and stronger than him as I was already catching up to him in height. I'd had my hair cut really short during the holidays before high school and it looked quite boyish and I was becoming fairly muscular the more I trained.

Our school was split into two sites – the Upper and Lower schools. Years One to Three were in the lower school and Four to Upper Sixth the upper school. The two schools were connected by a bridle path which Mum dropped me at after dropping Grace at the Upper School each morning so she could get off to work.

The Lower School was an imposing building in the middle of beautiful farm fields, with the obligatory track marked out on the field, which was so uneven that if you hit a hole in it when you were training your ankles could hurt like hell for ages afterwards. Looby and I used to circle the school a hundred times a day during break times just talking to each other and friends that we bumped into on the way round. She didn't really get on with Jane so we never really mixed with her at school. Besides it wouldn't really be fair to have gone and spoken to Jane as her mates would think she was so uncool to be friends with a first year.

Jane was going out with the lower school heartthrob Matt. Everybody fancied him, he was gorgeous. When he started coming round to her house in the evenings when I was there he brought his mate Paul with him. Paul was quite attractive in a 'pretty boy' kind of way. His hair was perfectly gelled to within an inch of his life and although he was quite shy when he did speak he had a mad sense of humour which I loved. He asked me out the third time he came round to her house and I of course said yes. It felt really good to be accepted by the older kids, as though I was safer than being just with kids my age. Besides I was quite mature for my age anyway and sometimes felt like I was older headed than these new friends.

Much to my regret now, I found myself neglecting Looby more than I should have and after going out with Paul for four weeks Looby and I had a huge row. I started to try to include her in my new friends but, like I said, she and Jane didn't really like each other so I made time for her as well and we eventually made up.

I found myself falling into puppy love with him, not that I was capable of real love at all, and the next time Jane and I went on a shopping trip we bought them both gold keyrings which said in glorious red scripted handwriting 'I Love You'. He told me he loved me too that night, after all it had been six weeks since we had started going out. Because he'd told me he loved me though he started to expect more from me. When he kissed me he used his tongue and I hated that. My jaw used to ache from the hours of trying to push his tongue back into his own mouth. Then he began to want to explore different parts of my body. I hated the fact that he wanted me to touch him because I didn't want to. Why did boys always want that? It was like they were normal and then all of a sudden a penis became involved and they turned into red faced leeches. I had been pushed so much as a child that I was determined that I wasn't going to be pushed again as, what I considered to be, a grown up! So I dumped him and asked for the keyring back. After all it had cost me £1.99 and I wanted to give it to someone that actually didn't want these things from me. Besides I didn't love him now. He'd made me feel uncomfortable and I hated him for that.

He brought the keyring back into school the next day and stood by the Goz Pit with it in his hand. The Goz Pit was a few steps in the bottom yard that led to a door that must have been for access underneath the school gym hall. Each time the ball went down the stairs and got trapped the cry of 'Goz Pit' would go up as everyone gathered round to see who would be brave enough to go down and get the ball whilst everybody spat at them – hence the name the Goz Pit!

So there he was with what I thought was my beautiful keyring in his hand, taking the mick out of me with all his mates because I wouldn't even let him to 'first base' calling me a kid He held out his hand with it in, I opened mine and into it he dropped the keyring all smashed up and mangled with Tippex all over the writing, but worst of all it was in a condom! I knew what condoms were because we had done sex education at school. The thought of what he'd given me made me gag. I ran off in tears to the toilets to scrub my hands. They felt as unclean as when Granddad had touched me and I scrubbed and scrubbed until the bell rang and I couldn't scrub anymore. When I came out of the toilets with my eyes red ringed from crying and my hands raw from scrubbing, Paul and his mates were outside the geography rooms waiting to go in. He looked at me and laughed as all his mates chanted Frigid at me. However, I knew I wasn't frigid, I knew that I'd already done things dirtier than they could ever imagine and I definitely wasn't going to give them the satisfaction of seeing me cry which was daft really because it was obvious I had been, I just didn't want them to see me dissolve. Over the next few weeks I began to toughen up a bit to their teasing and even starting giving a bit back but never too much because I was scared that they'd come after me again with more filthy things and I couldn't cope with that.

Jane and I began to drift apart when I phoned her at her friend Susie's house and Susie and Chloe, another friend of Jane's, were in the background shouting at me to piss off because I was a first year and they were third years. I was strong as hell, just saying 'whatever' before hanging up on their laughing. I dissolved into tears. For the first time in my life I had felt part of a group and a safe group at that and now it was all gone. They had just about confirmed what I felt about myself, that I was completely stupid and worthless. Of course, why would they want to be friends with me? Regardless of how old I felt in my head I was just a kid.

Jane was really apologetic when she next saw me, but the damage had been done and I had lost interest now. We still went training together,

Chloe sometimes came along with us, and Jay still came of course, but I couldn't forgive Chloe for how she had made me feel. Towards the end of my first year my friendship with Jane fizzled out.

I'd had other boyfriends but I tried to pick ones who were slightly more immature so they wouldn't know about the sorts of things that grown ups did. But I eventually succumbed to first base, then second, although I never quite lived down that time and Paul. I knew my life would get easier at the end of the school year because they would leave to go to the Upper School and my year would no longer be the babies. Someone else would get it and not me.

At night when I was alone in my room I used to take my compass and dig holes into my skin to let out this pain I was feeling. It felt so good to release some of that pain inside. I began to turn to that as opposed to my imaginary friend more and more. I was outgrowing him now, just as those girls had outgrown me. I wasn't as mean to him as they were though, I just only saw him when I absolutely needed him which meant he was free to go and help other girls who were scared of something. He was happy and so was I.

The second year came with a new set of rules. Like I said I had toughened up a lot and was beginning to accept a more laid back approach with the lads. If what they wanted was for me not to be frigid then I wouldn't be. I desperately wanted to shake the whole Paul situation, so I started to let them have what they wanted. It seemed to me that that was all boys or men really wanted anyway. Although not my Dad, my Dad was a gentleman and also a gentle man.

Looby and I were still close as anything for the first few months and then I started being really shitty with her, something I deeply regret now because I believe we could have been the best of friends for a long time. She was one of the only people at School who I'd felt had completely accepted me for who and what I was. The other person was Dan.

Dan was, and still is, my closest male friend. At the beginning of the second year we sat together in French, German and Maths because our surnames were next to each other alphabetically. Dan was the first boy I ever told my secret to, granted some years after this, but he was the first boy I ever trusted completely. He asked me out once in German, we had been told to do this exercise in the back of our books then swap for marking and he'd done the exercise but written next to it in big letters 'WILL YOU GO OUT WITH ME'. I marked his exercise and then wrote 'NO' in equally big letters next to it. Fortunately for us it never came between our friendship and we have remained till this day the best of friends. Dan had an uncanny knack of making me feel safe. He always knew what to say to me to make me smile. In my heart of hearts I don't know how I'd have got through some of my high school years without his support.

Then there was Davey Hesk. Dave was a sweetheart who saw the sadness behind the painted face of me. He used to walk home with me down the bridle path singing me songs in his gorgeous voice that could make me melt. Again there was never anything between us, we were just really good mates. We talked about our love life troubles and he used to confide in me about things that were happening at home between him and his parents. Mum used to call Dave 'Bart' because he had a flat head hair do like Bart Simpson and the deepest laugh you have ever heard. It was through Dave that I met my first proper boyfriend, Duncan.

To me Dunc was the most gorgeous boy in school. He was taller than me and of a slim build. He had really dark brown eyes and when he smiled his nose wrinkled up and his eyes went into a thin line, something that I found really cute about him. His mates were the cool kids at school so I became kind of cool by association. I went out with him for six months and at the end let him go all the way. Looby was with a friend of his, Hayden, at the same time. We had always vowed we would 'lose it' together, even though she didn't know that I'd already done it a thousand times. I don't remember much about it except that we used a condom so I didn't have to worry about the usual stickyness or the clean up. In fact it wasn't much to write home about at all (sorry Dunc!). I think both of us were very inexperienced and he didn't really have a clue what he was doing.

We split up about two weeks after that. I think he'd outgrown me but to me it felt like I'd put out and so he was off. I felt I'd been crap in bed and he'd decided that he was going to move onto the next girl, who was the most gorgeous girl in his year, Tracey.

Five weeks after that night, that I class as when I lost my virginity, when I still didn't have my period I was worried to death. I had confided in a friend of mine Angie, who in turn told a girl called Sian, who worked with my sister in the village newsagents. Sian persuaded me to go and talk to my form tutor, Mrs RR, as we called her because her name was double-barreled. Mrs RR was fantastic! I mean as a teacher she was wonderful anyway because she cared about us all and she had passion for what she did, but this particular time she was fantastic. She didn't judge me she just threw her arms around me and said that she'd help. She took me to the school nurse who arranged for a pregnancy test, which thank God came back negative, but not before the whole school had found out and Dunc had had a really big go at me for what he said was my fault. I never really spoke to him properly again after that. He had just confirmed what I had always thought, that most lads were a waste of space and that I wasn't worth spending with for them unless I'd put out. Mrs RR and I always got on well after that because I had so much respect for the way in which she had dealt with me. She had warned me about the dangers of unprotected sex and had said her door was always open if I needed to talk. I was desperate to tell her my secret because I knew she'd help but I didn't and I don't know why.

She was married to Mr Richards, one of the PE Teachers. I always got on well with him too. I think she had obviously told him about me and what had happened and the teachers all knew that the whole school knew and were calling me rotten. For once they all rallied round to keep me protected.

In the third year, being top of the school was great. I had started smoking and quite often bunked off lessons to go and sit either on the bridle path or in the stables, an out of bounds area next to the bike sheds near the front entrance to the school, to have a sneaky fag. I hung around with no-one in particular now. Drifting from group to group because I'd got a reputation for being a slag after the Dunc saga. It always seemed so unfair to me that I'd gone from being called frigid to a slag and yet to all the lads Dunc was a hero because he'd gotten a girl to give him what he wanted, what all the lads wanted. I thought well if they think I'm a slag anyway I might as well be and I began sleeping around, fuelling the name calling. I used sex as a hiding mechanism, to become accepted by the lads and to get some of the attention I craved. To have a lad hold me and want me so desperately became so messed up in my logic that I would think he would be the one who'd save me, who'd be the man at the window. When he turned out to be nothing of the sort I would just turn it into my hatred and disgust for myself and everything I stood for.

I also became a compulsive liar, frequently making up things to gain acceptance, of course neither of these things worked and just made my reputation worse.

One of the hardest parts for me was dealing with my feelings towards the male members of my class. I'd obviously had loads of boyfriends but no one had ever made me feel special, not that I wanted the 'special' that Granddad gave me, but special to them, the princess I'd always wanted to be. Most of the guys I went out with liked me because I was a sure thing. I found myself more and more attracted to some of the girls at school, particularly the older ones. They seemed to have so much self confidence and be able to look after themselves so much better than the girls my age. They strutted around the school like they owned it and I was obsessed by their strength and beauty.

I had always felt repulsed with myself after sex. I had never really enjoyed the way it made me feel. A friend of mine, who shall remain nameless as she is now married with children, kissed me one night taking me completely off guard. I mean we'd talked about it before, as most teenage girls do, but I'd never considered that it might happen. It was a kiss like I had never felt before, she was so gentle and tender. She had the most gorgeous silky skin and as her hands moved down to my breasts I didn't tense up like I had done with all of the lads that had touched me. Her body was really smooth and the way she smelt was mesmerizing. I was fascinated by the way she could make me feel, and for the first time in my life I enjoyed physical and sexual contact, not through penetration but the way she kissed and touched me. I never knew that a girl could make me feel so good, yet also feel so ashamed. I was turning into the bad girl but how come it felt so good. I was so confused? For the next few months we experimented with each other in every way we could, obviously keeping it our secret, until she decided that she didn't want to anymore. My heart was completely broken as I was convinced we would have been together forever as for the first time in my life I had felt something real, the kind of love that I hadn't experienced with the lads I'd been with, as the majority of them just used me because of my bad reputation. These feelings I had for her led to further confusion and isolated me from the other kids at school more and my self-loathing grew stronger each day. I found myself thinking about women more and more. The safety and security I had felt when she held me had been unlike anything I had felt before. However, I knew I had to suppress these feelings deep inside me, along with my secret because it would have just been another thing that the kids at school could have used to further damage my reputation or make my life more miserable. I struggled so hard to lose the feelings that I felt inside me for her that I couldn't really be friends with her anymore. It just didn't feel right.

There were so many things I hated about myself and that other people hated about me. I just felt more alone than ever.

The one trait I had developed that I was proud of was that the kids in the school used to come to me if they were being bullied. I couldn't stand bullying so I used to go and have a word with the person concerned, because I was so tall I always got it to stop and became quite popular with the younger kids in the school because of it. Whether it was physical, emotional or sexual bullying I couldn't tolerate it and would always be the first one in there to sort it out, never with violence just by talking to the kids involved.

Despite all this I did become a prefect and managed to hold onto the badge all year long. My reputation was damaged beyond all recognition. My parents would have hated me if they knew, the ironic thing being in a way his prophecy had become true, I had become the dirty girl that he always said I had been and all the lads in the school knew it. I generally didn't find it hard to get a boyfriend because of this. I was never short of male attention. I'd had a few longer term boyfriends but had always screwed it up by being so messed up inside and despite wanting to have someone get close to me to keep me safe I always pushed people away or cheated on them. As well as using it as a weapon to try to keep whoever the current boyfriend may have been I was almost hiding behind sex.

I'd been seeing a guy called Michael Burton at the end of the second year and I thought he was gorgeous. His family always made me feel really welcome. His sister was the same age as me although she was a lot less mature than I was. He didn't go to my school, he went to Manchester Grammar. He was intelligent, sweet and thoughtful. He was best friends with Christian, a guy who was in the year above me at my school and we had met in the local closed down mill, Slitten Brook where we used to go at night after the youth club to drink, smoke and listen to music. Michael and I became very close, very good friends and soon fell into teenage love, although I can't have loved him that much because I then dumped him to go out with his best mate from school who was a complete bastard! I was more used to being treated with disgust as Darren did, than nicely by a guy like Michael.

True to form Darren made my life a misery by cheating, lying and dropping me whenever he could. I mean don't get me wrong, I wasn't an angel to him. The fact that he lived 15 miles away from me made it easier to cheat on him without him finding out. I would have thought our incompatibility would have made me more wary but despite all of this he became the first boyfriend I confided in about my Granddad. He'd laughed at the time, because he'd had too much to drink, and said it takes some kind of slut to seduce her Granddad, but for some reason I stayed with him for 18 months. He had only told me what I'd thought about myself, so in my own way, I just accepted and stored what he said.

Darren was more messed up inside than I was. His Dad had died shortly before I met him and it had completely screwed him up. He had never forgiven himself for not being there, for going to a party to have a laugh the night he died. I had frequently counseled him telling him that he couldn't have known but he found it so difficult to live with the, wrongly apportioned, guilt over this. He wasn't as supportive for me. He came over to my Nana's house with me and got on famously with my Granddad. They sat at opposite ends of the sofa having a pint and talking like they'd known each other forever.

The night before my thirteenth birthday Dad and I had a huge row because I'd lied to him about something. I'd been out at a friend of mine, Kirsten's, house supposedly doing my homework but had gone to another mate, Ali's house instead and he was furious. When we got home Dad went to slap my face, something which he has never done in his life being so gentle, in an act of defiance I screamed something back and ran out of the room. He shouted after me that I was grounded. I'd been in trouble at school as well and my work was slipping again. I couldn't afford for it to slip anymore because I was just about to take my options at 13, a choice that would affect the rest of my life. I sat upstairs in my bedroom crying my heart out, hating every second of that night before my birthday, knowing that tomorrow I wouldn't even be able to go out and spend it with my mates to take my mind off the horrible memories that flooded back each year and I felt so desperately alone. I put a warm jumper on, picked up my cigarettes and lighter from my superb hiding place inside the hem on my heavy beige curtains, got some money out of my stash that I kept hidden underneath the fish tank on my dressing table and sneaked down the stairs. The tears were still streaming down my face as I turned the back door lock as quietly as I could and slid out into the darkness. I knew the front curtains would be shut because Mum hated the lights being on with the curtains open, everyone could see in. I crept out into the back garden, round the side of the house, stepping carefully over the hose pipe, round the corner and past the front of the house. I was running now, I didn't know where I was going but I was running. It was like one of the adventures with my imaginary friend. I had super human speed, my money jingling in my trackie bottoms slapping against my fags and lighter. I ran and ran until the sweat poured down the side of my face mixing with my tears, stinging my eyes. When I finally stopped I realized I was completely alone, my imaginary friend wasn't here, and now it was pitch dark.

The trees on Longbutt Lane that provided cover when we sneaked off from school for a fag didn't look so safe in this light. There he seemed to be hidden in every shadow. Tears were still streaming down my face and it was quiet, so very quiet. Inside my head I was screaming so loud I couldn't hear myself think but I didn't make a sound as I walked timidly up to the upper school and passed the shop where Grace bought the most delicious turkey mayo rolls in the world for her lunch.

They were made on long soft white batons and the owner smothered them in salad cream. They must have made hundreds of those rolls each day because everyone at school loved them. They packed them up in see through plastic thin bags that looked like freezer bags. I walked past the shop which was all locked up now, it wouldn't have mattered if it was open tonight, I wouldn't have gone in because I couldn't eat anything even though for once I had the money. I went to the pay phone to call a taxi. I wanted to get as far away from here as I could. That's when it hit me, I'd go to Darren. He would hide me, which of course was a great idea in principle until I knocked on his door after a twenty minute taxi ride to be met by his Mum in her nightie. They said I could stay overnight but that I had to phone Mum and Dad which I refused to do. As it happens his Mum had already phoned them from the other room and within twenty minutes they were on the doorstep. Mum flung her arms around me tears streaming down her face, her top already wet with her tears from the journey over. Dad didn't speak. My mind wasn't working properly, I thought I could make a run for it as they walked me out to the car but Mum wouldn't let go of my hand. Darren's driveway was long and dark and Mum was holding my hand so tight that it was white were she'd cut off the circulation and it was starting to hurt. I wanted my imaginary friend here. I wished I hadn't come to Darren. He'd let me down. I don't know why I'd thought he would be any different than the other guys who just used me for what they could get. I wished I'd got on a train instead of coming here and gone far away because now I had no escape. Mum and Dad hid all the keys when we got home and we sat whilst they talked at me for a while. I couldn't take anything in, all I could think of was that it had turned twelve o'clock and it was my birthday.

I just didn't want to face it, all day having to stay in the house. There would be no escape from my mind. Mum phoned school so that they made sure I didn't run off again and I was watched like a hawk all day. I couldn't concentrate on anything and turned to Dan to look after me. I told him everything that had happened and he was so supportive as he always was, we talked about telling someone why I had done it but I knew I wouldn't. Even Looby was supportive despite the fact that we'd fallen out so many times that year that we just weren't as close as we had been.

I sat in my room that night looking at the window. Mum and Dad had tried to make a fuss of my birthday with a cake but none of our hearts were in it. Grace had told me I was being pathetic but what did she know. I knew she didn't mean it really, she was hurt by my actions. I knew that she was just as concerned about me as Mum and Dad and was just hitting out, however to me it felt like another rejection. I just couldn't cope and as soon as everyone went to bed I sat making holes in my legs with my compass with tears falling silently down my face.

When I looked up I could see him which ever way I turned, smiling his wry smile and giggling in the same spooky way he always did. He was inside my head and there was nothing I could do. I squeezed each puncture hole to get as much blood out of each one because my blood was tainted with his touch, I was his flesh and blood therefore my blood was his. My legs were really sore by then and each tear that fell down my cheek and onto the tiny cuts stung like hell from the salt as it mingled with the thick red liquid making it runny and watery. As they dropped I could see the redness mixing, swirling into each tear. That is all I had left in me, blood and tears.

It felt good to make the pain physical though. God it felt good. Getting his blood out of me. I imagined that I could drain all the blood from my body to get myself clean again. Maybe this would work? Maybe this was like an exorcism?

I took a deodorant can and sprayed so close to my skin on my leg to burn it. The pain was intense and a big red welt appeared. Oh shit that would be visible; I hadn't expected it to work so well. I'd have to make up something about that for Mum and school because she'd notice and I was too ashamed to tell her the truth. The skin where I had burnt it looked red raw and scaly and it was oozing a clear liquid from the edges. I got a clean flannel from the airing cupboard and soaked it in cold water. This disturbed Mum and she was up and out of bed like a shot. I dived under the covers with my cleaning paraphernalia just as he did when he came to me and as she sat talking to me on the edge of the bed I wanted so desperately to talk to her about how I was feeling, what I was doing to myself and why, but I couldn't find the words. After she'd kissed me goodnight again I leant out of my bedroom window smoking and thinking about the day. Another birthday over and done with. Another set of memories that I would never be able to get away from. Why did I always make my birthdays so crap?

A few days later when things had started to return to semi normal again Mum noticed the burn. I told her I'd done it by accident on one of the radiators at school and she left it at that although it must have played on her mind because many years later when we finally talked about my self-harm and I faced it she brought it up and I told her what I had done. I didn't realize in any part of what I was doing that I was hurting her and Dad as well as myself. I suppose I only really understand it now I am a parent. The first time Lucie fell and cut her skin I was mortified to see her blood oozing out and a big welt appear on her perfect skin.

That spring and summer passed in a blur. All we talked about at school was our up coming exams and the options we had for our GCSE's. Finishing third year we would move up to the Upper School for the next year. Grace and I were going through our worst phase of arguing ever. She'd get out of the car in the morning and once she was out of earshot of Mum she'd call me a slut or a slag. What could I say to that, I was a slut! I had the reputation to prove it!

Darren had been unfaithful to me again with a girl called Cathy. Cathy in turn was going out with one of our Grace's friends, Martin. On the day that we went to find our feet at the Upper School he said hi to me. I'd heard that he liked me from a distance through Grace but I wasn't sure if it was just because his girlfriend had got off with my boyfriend and he wanted me as revenge.

Whether or not it was revenge, I don't know but we did get together, the final straw in mine and Looby's friendship because she fancied him also and he took her out for a while whilst I was messing about debating whether to finish with Darren. Darren had proposed to me when I was thirteen and I'd stupidly said yes, for all the wrong reasons. I thought him proposing would have me into safety, but of course he was abusive in the way he treated me so why I thought that I do not know.

After I did properly finish with Darren, Martin and I got involved in a big way. I told him everything about me and he was so supportive. He is the reason that the abuse stopped for me because once I'd taken him round to Nanas house and he stared and scowled at Granddad for all he was worth. Being 6ft 2 he was quite a frightening looking lad and did a fabulous job of intimidating Granddad. Granddad never touched me again.

Chapter 9

And Again

And then there was the parallel life I led through these years at high school, to that of painted faced Rachel. This life that I led behind closed doors, where I couldn't hide or run. Where I was loved by all my family, but violated so badly that I felt so desolate and alone.

Being at the high school was a challenge in itself without having to put up with the monstrosities I had to endure in my personal life. I managed to become two people – there was 'happy go lucky Rach', the eleven year old that wanted to desperately to fit in at school and be accepted not for being 'special' but just for being me, and then there was the other side, the damaged, gentle, abused, lonely side. The two rarely merged and if they did I pushed people away whilst running away from everyone around me who did actually care. Everyone except Dan. I pushed everyone away so that they wouldn't care and then they couldn't know me inside and see how ugly I really was.

I no longer cried as much when he came to me. I could sometimes control my tears for the duration until he'd left. They made no difference anyway and if he ever did see them he didn't care that he'd caused them until afterwards when he liked to hold me like a grandfather should or when he used to sit and talk about the war or tell me a story. He was so many different people rolled into one – the nasty drunk, the friendly drunk, the bastard, the doting husband, the miserable man, the fund raiser, the joker and the most evil, my torturer.

In my memory the times roll into one now. I think this is because it happened again and again I can no longer distinguish as well. Plus I went through such a period of denial where I blocked everything so well, locked it away in some part of my head that I just didn't want to visit, although it would still come out in my dreams.

Again. As he tiptoed across the bedroom and I disappeared to the window. I was almost as tall as my imaginary friend now. He was there waiting for me reaching out his hands so I could go into his chest and smell him instead of the cheap aftershave that clung to me after I'd been used for his pleasure. And as his fingers explored around inside my pants and he put his penis in my hand, my friend and I were running, playing with each other without a penis. We didn't need a penis to have fun. We chased each other flying through the air until we reached Lymm, my place of safety. We landed and ran down the old railway track to my secret place, the place that made his penetration disappear and not important to me.

It was beautiful in my secret place. This was the kind of secret I wanted to have inside me, the kind that didn't hurt. Some friends and I had discovered it when we had been riding down the old railway on our bikes one day. It was a flat bridge with horizontal wrought iron poles to prevent people from falling into the little stream that lay fifteen feet below. The bottom of the stream was littered with small pebbles which caught the reflections from the top of the water as it bubbled along. But the nicest thing about my secret little place was there was a gap just at the end of the railings and if you twisted around you could jump down onto the bank and crawl underneath the side of the bridge. It was a brilliant place for a den as it was so private. There was a Kingfisher that nested under there every year and it was the most beautiful thing I had ever seen. So all the time as he was pushing into my body and whispering into my ears I was jumping in the brook with my imaginary friend and the Kingfisher. I wasn't full of his pleasure, I was full of happiness to be in my secure fantasy world, in a place so familiar to me that I could almost let go and allow myself to feel numb and, dare I say it, almost safe.

It didn't last for long that time. He didn't last for long until he came on me. I always hated that bit the most when he came. I had done sex education at school and had learnt everything I needed to know. Everything apart from how to say no that is! I wish they'd taught me how to say no. I think it is something that desperately needs to be added into the curriculum, how to deal with sexual pressure, obviously not just from an abuse point of view, but for boys and girls in their teenage years who feel pressured into having experiences that their bodies may be ready for but that they have no capability emotionally to deal with. I had the vocabulary to be able to put what was happening to me into words now. I understood it and knew that it was wrong, but I was still too scared to tell and scared enough of him to let him do what he wanted to do, even though I knew that the police definitely wouldn't take me away. Mum and Dad loved her parents and it would destroy the whole family so how could I say anything to them. I didn't know which teacher would help me and there wasn't really any other grown up in my life that I trusted enough to turn to. So I did what I did best, kept it all inside.

And again. I was trapped. He'd pushed me into the alcove where the washing machine was housed in the kitchen and his whiskers closed over my mouth. I hated the way his moustache felt. Some people had soft whiskers but his were thick and wiry and made my face numb and red from where he kissed me. I couldn't see the window, which made me feel panicky and I could smell the whisky on his breath. He was pushing his lips into mine and I didn't want to breathe. I didn't want to smell the alcohol. I looked deep into his eyes to see if I could escape by pleading but he either didn't see my fear or chose to ignore it. Things had been normal all day, then Nana had decided to nip next door to see the lovely couple who lived there. They always made a fuss of Grace and I when we came and I had said to Nana I'd come but she said for me to stay at home. They had lived there for around about the same amount of time as Nana and had seen Mum and her sisters grow up before us. I'd heard whispers that one of them was fairly ill, the children weren't involved in any illness so I stayed home like I was told to. It didn't feel like home to me though. I was too far behind the wall with the vinyl tile effect wallpaper covering that separated the washing machine from the rest of the kitchen so I still couldn't see the window. I focused on the wrinkles above his eyes. There was one wrinkle that ran the full length of his forehead, then several underneath that split off half way across from each side, pointing down slightly as though to draw attention to his nose and then in turn the intent look in his eyes. His eyes would glaze over when he looked at me as though he were shutting down himself. Maybe he had an imaginary friend too who took him away from situations where he felt out of control. I didn't want to look in his eyes anymore and see Granddad, I wanted my Gramps back. I tried to switch off to the pain of what he was doing and I managed to do it for the physical side, however the pain in my chest through my heart thudding and the emotional pain that surged through my body as he had previously hit with a ferocious intensity. He pulled his hand out of my pants and there was blood on it. Oh God! This couldn't have been happening, my period had come. He looked down as if examining it and moved to the sink to wash his hands and I could tell he was furious. I was frozen to the spot not daring to move although he was just out of sight behind the alcove wall and I could hear the tap running as he scrubbed his hands. I wanted to move because I knew if I didn't that I would stain my pants with my period but I couldn't. I waited dutifully like the good girl I pretended to be until he gave me his permission to move. And when he did I went to my bedroom to get my sanitary towels and clean myself up all the while shaking because I knew he could come here at any moment. My pants were ruined with hot stickyness and I had leaked onto my jeans the zip open where he had had his hand momentarily before. I felt so dirty. I knew Nana wouldn't let me have a bath because I wasn't staying over tonight so I would have to wait until I got home. I was allowed to use the hot tap now though – I was a lot older and a lot more responsible. Inside I felt older than he was.

Mum was coming for me soon so I went back downstairs with my sanitary towels into the cold bathroom where the flannel he had used to clean me for a lifetime was spread out over the side of the bath. This particular day there was a massive spider in the bath. It looked so big it was staring at me with all eight eyes and almost flexing its muscles on which were huge tattoos!

I'd always been scared of spiders. Mum put it down to an experience I had in Canada at my cousin Sally's house in the middle of the Rocky Mountains. Mum had turned out the light to put me to sleep and I had screamed and screamed. When she came back into the room there was a Wolfshead Spider in the cot with me. They are perfectly harmless just very big. This one was around about the size of my head and right next to my face, so I can only imagine how scary and big it would have looked to me. Today though, a spider couldn't scare me. I had much more important things to worry about. Much bigger things!

He never penetrated me with his penis again after that day.

And again. His hand cupped around the back of my neck as he pulled my face to his. He liked to kiss me and look at me as he kissed me. I was embarrassed because I had started to develop breasts now which he loved to touch. He could spend ages just holding them in his hands, touching my nipples, so much so that for a while I couldn't bear any man to touch them Even now I sometimes have to open my eyes wide and concentrate fully on who is touching me when I feel insecure and I hate it if I cannot feel air on my face, if I am trapped. He guided my hand to his penis which was throbbing and erect waiting for my touch, waiting for me to get him more and more excited until it would be over and I could clean myself up, paint on my normal face and carry on with the day. He pushed my face down towards his open trousers. This was the bit I hated the most. I hated the feel of him on my face and I would scrub it almost red raw when everyone else was in bed at night with the clean flannels at home. Our flannels at home were clean and smelt fresh, not like the ones at Nana's which she could have bleached and they'd never have been clean to me.

After he had done he was always nice to me – as if the very satisfaction he took from it made the transition into the different person he was as Gramps – if it was during the day he would make a cup of tea and let me have some biscuits or let me have the television on in the living room. I had grown past playing with the ornaments on the fireplace and used to take a lot of books with me or sometimes my homework.

Books were another part of my escapism. I could get lost in a book and even though I was growing up, I still liked to go in my daydreams about me and my imaginary friend being the starring characters in the stories. My fantasy worlds were much nicer to be in and the very act of concentrating on each word and how each collection of words became a sentence, then a group of sentences transforming into a paragraph pulling me deeper into the plot within the story, I could almost forget my harsh realities.

I looked into the mirror at the mark on my neck where his fingers had dug in as he spurted onto my face. I could taste that vile taste in my mouth of what he had left there and it made me feel sick. Not even the tasty sandwiches that Nana would make for lunch would get rid of that taste. I couldn't describe it I just knew I'd never tasted anything so disgusting. I used to like to put tiny bits of bleach into my mouth and swill it around afterwards to clean my mouth properly but I could never do too much because it burnt like hell and made my tongue feel terrible but in a sick kind of way it made me feel better. I tried to drink bleach once because I knew I had swallowed some of him and I wanted to feel clean from the inside. I'd poured it into an Oldham Athletic Football Club mug – God only knows why we had that in our house being devoted Manchester United fans – and taken two big gulps. The pain that I'd felt was almost exciting as it hit the back of my throat. It was a physical pain not like when he left things in my mouth which just hurt my head but something that hurt for a reason. However, two seconds later I was violently sick, throwing up everything in my stomach including the bleach which I could feel, for days afterwards, had only reached just past my tonsils and my throat burnt like hell. In my own sick and twisted way though it felt good.

I was hurting myself quite badly at every opportunity out of sheer frustration and not knowing how to vent my anger. I'd started a lifelong cycle of blaming myself for everything and begun to exist on pure self hatred. The thing was I hated myself even more for scratching myself, digging knives, compasses, anything sharp I could find into my skin where no one could see, but I couldn't stop, the pain just felt too good, a physical outlet. Hiding this pain inside was really taking its toll on me, although on the outside I managed to remain fairly painted. The cutting went on well into my twenties whenever I couldn't cope and was really difficult to get under control. I wanted so badly to be able to cut out bits of skin he had touched.

I would go for weeks starving myself until my ribs stuck out because I knew if I did and he hurt me I would bruise. The bruises made it physical. They made me believe what was happening to me because sometimes in my own little fantasy world I could convince myself that this wasn't real. The bruises helped me to deal with the reality which I needed to do in my own way. They also meant someone might ask me what was wrong. Not that I'd tell anyone as I was still too scared, but it would be nice to be asked.

And again. He was sitting on the sofa and Nana was in the bath. He'd started to let me have a glass of his home made wine in the evening which was nice because it numbed any pain I felt. In fact it numbed everything, my sense of danger, my sense of awareness, it just completely relaxed me. I was in front of the fire doing some homework. It was my favourite place to be there because it was so cosy. The hearth was made of yellow tiles and the fire was an old gas one that Nana sometimes had to light with a match if the ignition was playing up which it did frequently. As his hand cupped my breasts I stared hard into the fire. The curtains were closed and I couldn't see the window, I had no escape. My eyes were stinging with the heat that was blasting as he circled each nipple through my top then underneath with his wrinkly hands. I was determined not to cry but my eyes stung so badly with the dry heat that water was streaming down my face. My bear was watching. Even though I was too old to play with him now I still liked to hold him in my hands every now and again. He was like a security blanket he was always cold being made out of brass.

And then Nana was out of the bath and he was back on the sofa leaving me with my liquid stained flushed cheeks. Nana suggested that I slept in her room with her that night because he had started sleeping in the back room so as not to be disturbed by her snoring. She was my saviour without even knowing it! I knew tonight I would be safe because Nana's door was always locked!

I never stayed in either the front or back room again.

The opportunities he had to touch me were becoming fewer and fewer as I no longer had to go there as much now. I was beginning to move away and he knew it. I could almost see the sadness in his eyes and that gave me such a sense of power over him. I knew that one day soon he would never be able to touch me again. I didn't realize quite how soon though.

I'd taken Darren over one weekend to meet them. Gramps had been feeling really ill although no-one had actually said so far what was up with him. I had just found out that he'd had to go to the hospital for some tests and I was concerned. It's really hard to explain how much I still loved that side of him. I think because I'd split myself into two people, it had given me more clarity on how he was able to be two people also. I was beginning to understand how two sides of a personality could be so different because I was morphing into the same sort of two people he was. The happy side, a person who people came to to talk their problems through and who always had a smile and then the darker side, secretive, angry and alone in my feelings.

Nana and Gramps loved Darren, although Mum and Dad weren't too keen. All they saw was a guy who was a couple of years older than me, who seemed to be a terrible influence, who drove a knackered out old banger of a car and made their baby cry frequently, so I can understand their reasoning, particularly now as a parent. God I will be devastated when Lucie brings home her first unsuitable boyfriend, of which I'm sure there will be many if she is anything like me!

Gramps gave him a beer as we hadn't driven, we'd come on the bus, the 500 from Altrincham. We had walked through the precinct and I'd told Darren all the stories and memories that I had from my childhood there. We'd walked past the pub with the, infamous in my family, wall that had more glass either side each time I saw it. The graffiti on the side of the pub got more obscene each time as well and this particular day there were a bunch of kids, probably about my age, spraying on their obscenities about some local girl who obviously put out easily.

Nana had made Spam butties and a fresh pot of tea which was keeping warm under the patchwork tea cosy in the kitchen for when we wanted our next cup. I didn't want any wine today. I couldn't understand why Darren was being so fine with Gramps. I mean he was at his full charming self that day but Darren knew everything and he didn't even flicker. I honestly believe he didn't think I was telling the truth and that hurt like hell, almost as much as the abuse itself. Instead of being angry with him it just made it more difficult for me to talk to anyone for fear of not being believed.

On the way home he was slightly tipsy and very quiet. I think it was the beginning of the end of our relationship and although he held me as I cried on the top deck of the bus I knew his heart wasn't in it.

The following week he cheated on me with Martin's girlfriend. He didn't sleep with her or so he told me and they were old friends so that in his eyes made it ok.

The next time I went to his house I saw a note he'd written in code on the calendar DDNLRA. He'd tried to disguise what it meant but he underestimated my imagination because I'd got it straight away - Darren does not love Rachel anymore. I confronted him and when I went to the toilet he locked himself in his room jamming some boxes behind the door. Despite our early troubles I got on well with his Mum because she knew he talked to me about his problems and I kept her in the picture when he was feeling really bad. I heard her shout him and shot downstairs. He had jumped out of the window and was legging it off up the street. I explained what had happened through floods of tears, but I think it was one too many times I'd cried over him. I pushed my way into his bedroom to get to my handbag so I could go and find him and there on the side was a letter written to his cousin at University talking about how he had slept with another girl shortly after I'd gone home the previous week. We had also slept together that day and I felt so utterly used and horrified that I took the letter downstairs to show his Mum. I said I'd find him and bring him home but that that was it. His sister, Lydia, was really upset because I got on really well with her too. After about an hour of searching I found him hiding in the cricket pavilion in Walton Road park and took him home. I left that day with my head held high. I mean don't get me wrong I'd done horrible things to him too, I'd slept with other people, I'd been unfaithful emotionally as well as physically, I'd done everything he'd done, but in my own mind I had taken enough from him and I wasn't about to be pushed around again.

I was pushed around again for the next six months though. I kept on going back for more even when Martin was waiting patiently for me. Martin had started seeing Looby and we had had a massive falling out because of it. All parents loved Martin because he was a nice guy. They seemed to trust their daughters with him and mine were no exception. Mum in particularly loved him. I think he was her favourite of the boyfriends that I'd had up to that point, although that just doesn't do him enough justice really as my choice in men had been rather rubbish to say the least.

Christmas came and went and on New Years Eve Martin gave me an ultimatum. It was either Darren or him. I picked him.

I will forever be thankful that I chose Martin but that I didn't marry him because we weren't good for each other. I brought out the worst in his jealous streak and he was quite controlling with my clothes, where I went and who I was friends with. Don't get me wrong, I wasn't the perfect girlfriend, old habits died very hard. We just didn't fit together properly and weren't suited. However, I will always be thankful to him for stopping the abuse. He single handedly dealt with it in a way that I had waited for someone to do all my life. He was my hero, the guy I could tell anything to and he didn't judge me, but most of all – in the beginning – he treated me with respect.

Chapter 10

The Diagnosis

My bedroom in the house in Lymm was lovely. Mum and Dad had had built in wardrobes fitted, they were made of a grey vinyl covered chip board and ran the full length of the left hand side of my room. The walls were wood chip and were painted in a soft white with a hint of pink in it and the carpet was grey. My bedding was turquoise with bright coloured shapes over it and it was the prettiest room of all of my friends because it was modern and bright. Except to me it was dirty. Everywhere I looked I could see his face. At night when I couldn't sleep my mind would play tricks on me and I would see him sitting at the pull-out desk half way along my wardrobe. I'd see him walk past my room and look in, shadowy from the landing light. I'd see him creeping across the room in his two tone pyjamas ready to climb into bed with me. I saw him everywhere.

He had recently become more ill and had been into hospital for a few tests, although no one seemed to be saying what was wrong with him.

I was working on an essay for my History teacher about Elizabethan England and I was finding it really hard. I was into daydream territory. I quite often just sat at the mirror above by desk looking at my face, just looking, trying to figure myself out, to no avail.

I had a picture of Martin on my mirror, only a small one and if it got too much to think about everything or I could see Granddad's face every-where, I could look at Martin's picture and it made me feel better. In the picture he was wearing a black and white jacket that I'd bought when I'd been to Afflecks Palace in Manchester, from a shop called Smith and Jones and it was my favourite, particularly after he'd worn it because it smelt familiar, safe.

I'd loved Afflecks Palace from the minute I first went in there. Darren took me one Saturday and I was a convert from then on. It was filled with the most exotic of smells, probably pot from what I remember, and it had the coolest shops you could imagine. They sold second hand 501's and gorgeous suede coats, of which I bought a beige one and thought I was the dog's dusters. Upstairs, there was a little market place that housed little stalls, one off pieces from fashion students and all manner of weird and wonderful trinkets, from the normal sparkles and sequins of the fashion of the time to the mad choice goth outfits that were available. I loved that little space. You could smoke as you were walking round browsing at what everybody had to offer.

Across the road there was the most fantastic vinyl shop. It was owned by the guys from 808 State. Being a Manchester music freak I could spend hours in there just flicking through the vinyls, the smells intoxicating and the sounds blasting out into the street mixing with the smoke from a thousand fags and spliffs. I'd once been sitting on the side of the street outside an arcade, I was going through my scruffy, black haired gothic faze, and a guy had walked past and given me 50p for a cup of tea! Then there was the time that I'd seen the homeless guy just up from Afflecks in Piccadilly Gardens. It was the middle of winter and he was sat on a bench shivering in his t-shirt, a scruffy old battered, once white, t-shirt. And here was me walking through in my wooly jumper and a leather jacket so I gave him my jumper. He was so grateful that tears welled up in his eyes. I'll never forget that, that look, he told me I was an angel. I wished for that one second I could be. I wished I could believe him. Darren had gone mad when I told him saying that he'd probably sell it to buy a few pints, but I didn't think he would. I thought he'd just stay warm for a change. I hadn't wanted to give him money as I wasn't so naïve to think he would buy a meal with it. I knew all the guys around there were drunks and would sell their souls for the next bottle or fag.

I was madly into the Stone Roses, the Inspiral Carpets and the Happy Mondays and always had some kind of music coming out of my bedroom. Grace was into dance music and most of the charts which just didn't appeal to me and it was a daily competition to see who could play their music the loudest, the other complaining to Mum that 'she won't shut it up and I'm trying to work' or 'hers is louder than mine', which usually led to the plug being pulled on both stereos and two very sulky teenagers. Grace and I both secretly thought that each other were the coolest thing, although we still hated each other!

All my posters had come down off my wall the minute I'd turned 13 when I deemed that I'd grown out of them.

The windowsill was high in my room and my window was a large one that opened from the bottom outwards. I quite often hung out of there having a fag at night, throwing my finished butts over the hedge and fence at the side of the house. How Mum and Dad never knew I smoked was beyond me because the road was littered with loads of fag ends that we sometimes blamed on the other kids in the neighbourhood. I loved sliding myself onto the wooden ledge in between the overlap of the fitted wardrobes and the window to sit on my pillow at night when I couldn't sleep. Instead of leaving my body in bed I could physically take myself to the window and feel the fresh air on my face, and instead of flying with my friend in my fantasy world I read books and did my homework in the dead of the night from there whilst everyone else slept. Consequently I was always tired at school and frequently didn't go in faking illness just so I could stay there in my room, in my place.

Sitting at my desk I used to dream of when I'd be old enough to have my own place, a flat, somewhere where I didn't have memories of my Granddad. He wouldn't be allowed there. I wouldn't let him come over physically and I certainly wouldn't let him be there in my head.

I knew something was going on and it kept me that day from doing my homework again. I couldn't concentrate on Elizabethan England when there were more important things to worry about. How was this important when my family was in turmoil?

Mum came in to talk to me, I knew it had to be bad for her to come into my room because she hated it in here, it was so messy. She sat on the edge of my bed and I turned to face her. I could see she had been in tears, I wanted to hug her but I didn't, I just sat and looked as she told me he had Cancer. I felt numb. Not sad, not scared, not relieved but numb.

She explained what Cancer of the Prostate meant. He'd been peeing blood and that's why he had had tests. It wasn't good, they hadn't caught it early enough to treat and he would be going back into hospital to spend some time having some treatment to see what they could do for him.

Inside I felt nothing for a few hours and then, much to my disgust, I felt laughter welling. I felt happy. I felt as though revenge was being dealt. But most of all I knew that that was it. He couldn't touch me again. Cancer meant he couldn't touch me. He would be treated and he'd get weak and I would be in the position of strength. After the laughter, I felt sad. Sad for the loss to the community, this great guy who did so much for the Legion. Who would do it now? Who would be the father figure of the family when Frank was gone? He was the oldest. Who would take over? Would it be my Dad? Or maybe his brother because he was older?

That night lying in bed I finally cried and once I started I couldn't stop. This time I cried for me. I cried for all the times he'd crept across the floor. I cried for all the times Martin had touched my breasts and it had made me feel sick because it reminded me of what had happened. I cried for all the times as a young child that I'd wanted to sit on his knee after he'd done what he wanted, and I'd wished that we could have just skipped the half an hour before that moment when he would be so tender and so caring, as a grandfather should be. I cried for the times that we'd painted together, that I'd helped him in the garden with the sweetpeas or the roses. I cried for the memories of cleaning Nana's spoons and them never actually feeling clean in my hands, because my hands were dirty, covered in memories of him although I couldn't see any marks on the skin. I cried because I felt helpless, powerless to control what was happening to him and also to me. I cried to get the pain out of my body. I cried because I wanted to split my skin, to feel blood flowing down my arms, my neck, my legs, to get the pain out. I cried because that's how he made me feel, desolate, dirty and alone. I cried because I'd not believed in God for a long time, but now I felt that he was getting his punishment, God was sending his wrath down through 'the penis'. I cried because I'd made that happen, because I'd wished and wished for something to make it stop and now, it had. I cried because I was guilty, because I was going to hell for letting him, being there, watching him touch himself and touch me in places I didn't want him to, but I still let him and I was as guilty as he was. Most of all I now cried for my Gramps. I cried for all he'd miss because deep down inside, I knew he would be the first person in my lifetime in my family to die and it would be my fault.

I hadn't had a lot of experience with death. The year before Mum had gone to Canada to see her sisters and Dad, Grace and I had waited until the end of that particular school term before going to the Isle of Man for a few days. One the last day of school Jay, who I'd trained with at Warrington Athletics Club and hung out with on the park at Outrington, had walked me home. Jay was friends with Mubsey, who I'd fancied at the time. Mubsey was going out with Carla, a girl in my year, a friend of his sister, who was also in my year, but that didn't stop me flirting like hell with him as usual. Jay had also been out with Jane for a while and they had remained friends because they trained together. We used to pick him up in Jane's Dad's Capri on the way. He was a fantastic runner and a great friend to have because he always had a smile and something funny to tell me. He didn't think of me as younger, like Jane and her friends had, he accepted me for who I was. He was kind and gentle although he was very strong from all the training he did. At the school sports days he held most of the records and his name was spread out over the printed sports programme every year.

He walked me home from school down the road that was opposite where I lived and we sat on the wall at the bottom. We'd been talking about all the things that we were going to do over the holidays, I was telling him about the Isle of Man and he was telling about going to Wales with Mubsey, his sister and their parents. I told him to send me a postcard (which I still have in my box of memories) and said I would send him one although his trip sounded much more fun than mine. They would be staying in tents and surfing which sounded really cool. Whereas we would be staying with friends on the Island and surfing wouldn't even come into it. We had tried surfing, Grace and I, one year in Newquay. We were both crap but we'd given it a go, under no instruction obviously, just the watchful eye of Dad. It sounded so fantastic that he would learn properly.

As I left I gave him a hug and we parted with promises of postcards, sticks of rock and all the stupid things you say before you leave a friend at the end of term to go on holiday.

We had a fab time in the Isle of Man, regardless of the 'no surfing', and when we got back the house smelt all musty from being locked up for so long with the weather being so sunny. I'd caught the sun and felt all posh with my new tan.

My postcard was waiting there for me, when I got home, telling me 'Wales isn't a "puma bag", but it's ok!'. Dad decided we'd get a takeaway for tea, phoned it through and waited for the obligatory ten minutes before setting out in the car to pick it up. Whilst we waited the news was on. There was Jay's face on the news, the recent school photograph he'd had taken, with his cheeky grin. Him and Mubsey had been swept out to sea by a freak wave, Mubs had managed to climb up some rocks on a cliff face, but Jay hadn't. They never found him, I found him here on Granada Reports, through my tears.

I don't know who it was but somebody once told me that you don't realize how much you cared about somebody until they were dead and this was so true. I went over my last conversation with him in my head time after time. If I'd known I'd not have talked about postcards, surfing and ironically swimming, but I'd have told him that I was so grateful for his friendship and that his smile sometimes brightened a really dark day for me.

I couldn't eat my Chinese as Dad had got the paper and of course it was all over the front cover, with the same photo, smiling back. I'd walked over the road in the evening to the playing fields there, with the stream that ran around the outside and eventually led to the magical place my imaginary friend and I had visited so many times. The stream eventually curled around from my place to a little bridge that you walked over to get to the cut through across the golf course. I sat on the bridge and cried, selfishly at first, then for Jay, all the while my sweaty hands holding my postcard.

After that week in the Isle of Man, Nana came to stay because Dad didn't have anymore time left to take off from the bank. She was there for us when we went to school and when we came home for a week until Mum got back from visiting her sisters. I was so depressed but I couldn't express it. One night I sat there in the box room, so terribly low. That's when I got the idea of taking tablets. Mum and Dad always had Paracetamol in the cupboard opposite the archway in the kitchen and as I sat there and took about 20 believing honestly that this would do it and I could die too. Maybe then people would question why and maybe they would love me more at school, just as I'd thought about Jay. Perhaps they would hold a memorial and people would say they missed me, that it was a tragic waste. However, all the paracetamol did was make me throw up and feel really shitty for the next few days. I was more miserable than ever and more alone because I'd felt sure this would have worked. Then I could find Jay again with his smile that cheered me up. I had to be content with spending a day off at home with Nana fussing around me as I threw up again and again. I had no energy at all.

I couldn't believe that God would take Jay, that he could be dead and that we wouldn't take me, someone who really wanted it. Jay didn't want to die. Nothing further from the truth, he was full of life and so strong. And now God was going to take Gramps as well!

My relationship with God had been a strange one really. I mean I'd been to Sunday school every week for the three years we'd lived on the Island for and I'd believed in God then. I knew God showered his subjects every now and again, to show them who was boss and in my own way I believed that Granddad had been acting for God because he was trying to save me, the same as the Sunday School Teachers had taught me Jesus had tried to save his disciples and all the bad people in the world. The more I learnt though, the more Sunday School taught me, the more I questioned to myself how God could let bad things happen. Why he could turn a blind eye to me when I needed his support to help me get through something hard. Why he let me have an imaginary friend with no penis? I still believed though until we moved back from the Island. When I realized that what was happening to me was wrong I stopped believing in God, I didn't believe God could create someone so monsterously horrible, yet on the other side so kind, gentle, funny and sweet.

Now I believed in God. He was raining down his wrath on 'the penis' by making it spew blood, like when Jesus turned the water to wine. And the worst part was it was my fault. Even though I didn't go to Church anymore, I didn't even pray out loud, sometimes in my head I had asked for help. If God heard everything and controlled his vengeance, then he'd answered my help. But he'd broken my Nana's heart, hurt my Mum, upset my Dad and the rest of my family, and for that I felt my skin would burn in hell.

The hardest part of that to deal with was the thought of my skin burning excited me in a way I couldn't explain, that I couldn't vocalize to anybody, because no one knew how it felt to be me inside. I'd lived with this internal pain for the majority of my life and I couldn't ever remember it not being there.

The next day was the first time I ever burnt myself with a cigarette. I thought if I was going burn in hell anyway I would start the job for them.

Over the last few years I had developed a really strong friendship with a girl that had moved from a nearby school because her Mum and her Mum's boyfriend lived in Statham which was just on the outskirts of Lymm. It was easier for Kirsten to go to my High School than the other local High School, because she didn't have to get a bus. Kirsten's Mum was a Social Worker at the council although I didn't quite know what she did. Her boyfriend, Neil did something in IT I think. Her Mum seemed really cool because she looked dead young and went out with a guy half her age. Kirsten had an older sister and two brothers, one younger, one older. They were a really nice family.

When I got to school I told Kirsten about the diagnosis and she was so supportive. I hadn't told her about what had happened yet. The only people that knew that counted were Dan and Martin, and they'd both been brilliant. I'd told a few other people in a drunken stupor in the park one night, but no one really understood and thought I was just pissed, rambling on. Besides like I said I'd lied about other things to try to be accepted, so why should anyone believe me about this?

Martin was brilliant again, a source of real support to me, but also to Mum. She could see I was going well off the rails, hitting out at everyone and thing I touched, and she could talk to him and find out if I was ok. Of course he was sworn to secrecy by me. He'd promised he wouldn't tell anyone and he knew he only got one chance with a promise with me.

Inside me the guilt grew more and more each day. I made sure that I tried to help with Nana because she was finding it really hard to cope with him being in hospital. Jill had come over to visit to see how he was and she was staying with us. She always stayed in my room and I was moved into the box room which was barely big enough to house the chair bed that I slept on. I always felt slightly resentful that Grace wasn't asked to move out of her room when people came to stay, why was it always me? I suppose in my own mind it made me believe more that I wasn't worthy of having my own space, I belonged in that room with the dirty laundry basket, because of course I was dirty, not just with Granddad but with so many people now I'd lost count. I'd been so easy to have and now this was another form of punishment.

I threw myself into helping Nana as did the rest of the family, Julie had come over from Canada and was staying at 172, Nana's house. She'd surprised Granddad by walking into the ward one day with us and just shouting 'Hey Frankie!' as she always did. He'd cried when he saw her knowing that she had no money, but that she'd come because he was ill. We all waited for news from the hospital each day, when it came it wasn't good. We knew for certain he was going to die.

Jill and Julie both went home to Canada and Mum was left to deal with all the crap that came with Cancer. I've never understood the extent of the things she had to deal with and I don't think I ever will.

I hated myself so much for what I had done. I could see everyone in my family going through so much pain, suffering and worry and it was all down to me.

When he came out of hospital he spent a while at home, until the blood came back as he went to the toilet and it was a bad sign. The single bed was in the living room now and it was becoming harder and harder for Nana to cope with having him at home.

I became even more of a loner at school. I drifted around from group to group of kids never getting settled because I knew that I wouldn't be accepted in the long term because I was wrong, dirty, a slut. I eventually ran out of groups in my year to hang around with as I'd neglected them so much the previous year when Martin had been at the school and I'd spent every second of my spare time with him, so I started to go into the art rooms at every available opportunity. Mr Giles, my art teacher, was an inspiration to me. He let me just get on with it, he never complained that I spent so much time there and I channeled my energies into my drawing and painting, experimenting with as many mediums as I could to get my final product, my exam pieces that would be graded for my GCSE result. I found it so therapeutic. I was writing a lot as well, deep poems, full of darkness, and the black that I felt inside.

When he became too ill to be cared for just by Nana and the District Nurse, he had to be admitted to a hospice and we all knew that he was going to die soon. The hospice was a square shaped building with a communal garden in the centre for relatives and friends to gather. There were four side rooms on each side and one larger ward in the middle. The entrance hall almost looked like the entrance to a church because it had a notice board with thank you cards and brightly coloured pieces of paper with notes of remembrance scrawled, some covered in the tears of family. There were six beds to a bay and all were full until someone went, then the curtains were drawn as the Undertaker came with his big silver trolley on wheels to take away 'the body', such a sad way to leave when they generally arrived by taxi or by ambulance to such a warm welcome from the fantastic staff. It struck me how sad it was that all these beds should be full of people just waiting to die and then there were the people waiting to getting in the bed of the person who just died to die themselves. Life didn't seem fair to me, like they were queuing outside with only their morphine drips and hallucinations for company. Only when they were deemed sicker than the next person were they allowed access into this inner sanctuary where the Occupational Therapists taught them how to make place mats and weave baskets, to be left as a reminder of the worst part of their illnesses for their families, when they were taken out in their own personal cold tin box.

Nana was feeling the strain of things, trying so hard to stay cheerful for our sake. Christmas was coming and the staff of the hospice had tried so hard to brighten up the rooms, when in essence they were greyer than the market, where my favourite sweet shop was, despite being beautifully decorated. I missed many a day off school, traveling the dreary journey between Altrincham and Wythenshawe, then through to Heald Green to be with Nana and sit at his bedside. I'd put it to one side, and was trying to make amends with God by being there for him and talking to him. I watched him do his crafts with the same concentration he had once applied to me and my body. That same look in his eye.

Then the morphine got stronger, and he got weaker and paler, his skin taking on a translucent palour. He found it hard to lose his control and fought having a catheter, but there came a time when he couldn't fight it any longer because he was no longer able to stand for a length of time and I'm ashamed to admit to see him cry as he filled the bag made me feel both elated and horrified. He hated it and he had no control and that made me feel stronger than him, however with my strength came more guilt than he could ever feel.

One Friday we were alone in the room in the hospice, Nana had gone to get a cup of tea and some fresh air. She loved the flowers in the front entrance garden. They had little signs next to them stating who had donated them and in whose memory. She'd always liked that. She'd spent hours in cemeteries reading the grave stones, fairly macabre but she loved it, or maybe it was the flowers, I don't know. We were alone. I sat looking at him and was filled with anger. I was so angry that I could feel the blood rushing around my body. I wanted to kick him, punch him, shake him, instead I sat in my cheap orange plastic chair and listened to him bumble his hallucinations into thin air. I looked deep into his lost eyes and my anger grew. He got morphine to kill the pain. What did I get? I got nothing. He got to live in a hallucinogenic world, anywhere he wanted to be, and I was stuck here, full of guilt, pain and anger with no outlet but to turn it on myself. I pushed my hands underneath my backside and they were so sweaty that the skin hurt as it stuck to the chair. When I took them out they were covered in tiny nobbles, the imprint that ran all the way across my white, sweaty palms, just as the couch had been imprinted on my face and the wallpaper pattern on my cheek when he'd finished. These patterns were everywhere and they made me feel sick to the stomach. Bile rose in my throat as I examined the dents in my skin. My eyes rose to his and for that second I know he saw me and I know he knew it was me, not some hallucination.

'Apologise' I said. 'Apologise to me'.

However his eyes had gone again, whether it be through choice or medication or whether he just couldn't deal with it. I never went again on my own, just with Mum and Dad when I had to.

We went on Christmas Day, Grace and I smiling fakely for the cameras with our cream skinned, translucent, shadow of a Gramps. No longer was he tanned and always giggling. Now he looked vacant, as vacant as the smiles on our faces.

I went to stay with Nana frequently to help. I stayed in the room with her, lying at night listening to her snore and the ghosts in the house of my past. All the time she snored felt like danger, I knew if she snored she was deeply asleep and that's when he came. I could see myself as a child playing with her clothes and jewelry, dressing up in front of the mirror in her room and imagining I was a movie star. I could see Grace and I playing in the garden with our toys. I could see Whisky asleep with one eye open as if to protect himself from some hidden evil by being alert even in sleep. If I did sleep Granddad was everywhere, I was filled with fear and the smell of him in my nose. When I was awake which ever way I turned he was there so I couldn't win, but still I insisted in going to stay. I suppose going there felt like my penance, another way to feel the pain and make it physical, it was the scratchy vest that in my head God made me wear each day for what I'd done.

Martin hated me going because he knew for weeks afterwards he would have to hold me as I cried, although I never explained to him why, he accepted that I felt I had to do it, but hated it all the same. Even his shoulders wrapped around me whilst I cried couldn't take away the pain or make me feel safe, because even though I knew he couldn't touch me anymore, he was in my blood, the same blood that flowed faster around my body when I saw him in my room, in the house, at Nana's, on every corner of every street and the same blood that I loved to see oozing out of my skin when I dug the sharp cold metal of a knife or implement into my body to get this pain out from inside me.

Chapter 11

The Death

It was coming up to my mock fourth year's exams and I was dreading them because I'd missed so much school. I was always skiving or talking Mum into letting me stay off. She knew I'd always struggled with my emotions and when Martin wasn't there I didn't really have a reason to go in. I didn't really fit in with any particular group, so why bother. There was one teacher at school who really had it in for me, my English Teacher. She hated me, and she hated my work. My essays took a real dive in grade when I got her. My former English teacher, Mrs Burton, had given my all the tools to express myself, but more than that she'd given me encouragement, help, suggestive thoughts and constructive criticism. This woman just made me hate the work, which was a shame because we were studying Anthony and Cleopatra which is a beautiful story and I've always had a love of Shakespeare, just not the way she presented it. She told me I wouldn't amount to anything and that I ran to hide behind my Mum when things got tough. I was mad at her because I should have run to Mum if I couldn't sort something out for myself. Thing is to me that was Mum's job. She spent so much time in school fighting my corner with this particular teacher and then subsequently the Deputy Head after that. The situation culminated in a stand up argument in the middle of the lesson, to which I stood up, told her to fuck off and walked out as she was shouting that again I was running to hide behind my Mum. God knows there were so many things I couldn't say to my family, this was so trivial compared to the bigger picture of my life. She just made it more miserable at school for me, which in turn meant the days I had English were generally the days I 'wagged' or faked illness for Mum.

I was at Kirsten's house that particular night, 25th January 1991. I had called Dad to ask if I could stay later, he'd said no and that he was coming to pick me up and I think in my heart I knew. I got into the car with Dad and for once I wasn't angry at being told I had to come home. Mum was still at the hospice and I didn't want to create any more stress than I already had done for them for once.

'Is he actually going to die?' I asked in the car.

'I think so love' Dad replied.

As soon as the door shut behind us Dad took me into his arms, he smelt familiar and his voice was muffled and broke into my hair as he told me that my tormentor was dead. I felt nothing. I think I squeezed two tears out for show purposes really, but inside I felt nothing.

When Grace got home Dad had the same conversation with her and for once I felt close to her. I sat next to her on the brown suede sofa in the living room and held her hand as she looked into the fire, silent tears rolling down her cheeks one by one. I sat there counting them, seventeen in total and I thought one eye must be sadder than the other because more tears came out of that one. I could see the reflection of the fire in her eyes, glistening still with water, but unable to unload it as she sat in her stunned silence. I just sat there too, holding her hand. It was cold, as if she were in shock. Grace, like me, obviously hadn't had much experience with death. Well we'd lost a rabbit many moons ago. Dad had brought us both into the house, much like this night, and told us that 'little Fluffy had gone to Rabbit Heaven'.

'Do you mean its dead' I'd piped up.

'Yes' Dad had replied.

'Can I touch it' I'd said!

Dad had laughed himself stupid over this. He'd thought we'd be gutted but we were typical inquisitive children. When we'd gone outside to see 'little Fluffy' in his finally resting place, a black bin bag on top of some cut grass, I'd given it a prod and said 'It's all stiff!' And that was really the sum of Grace's experience of death, apart from a few goldfish on the way and when Nana's cat, Whisky, had died, which I'd actually been quite happy about at the time because he would no longer look at me, my secret in his smug eyes.

As Dad held me before I went to bed, I drank in again his familiar smell. Dad was everything that personified my safety, Mum too. I wouldn't be able to sleep until Mum got home, because deep down I knew that this was her Dad that had died, someone she'd never be able to smell again. She'd never seemed as close to her Dad as I was to mine though. He'd been very strict with them as children, dare I say it even cruel and I don't think she'd ever forgiven him fully, although it was probably made easier because he adored his grandchildren and we all adored Gramps.

I watched for Mum coming home, sat on the windowsill, in my safe sanctuary. When her car pulled round the corner of the lane that lead to my house I took a deep breath and prepared myself for the things I needed to say to her because her Dad was dead.

I heard her key go in the door and I heard Dad go to help her in. Within a few minutes she was sat in my room on the side of the bed, just as she had sat when she had told me he had Cancer. Only now it was different some-how. She looked tired, emotionally drained and small. Mum had always been so strong, even when she was crying, but she looked beaten now. I listened to her tell me how it had happened, how she'd told Nana and Jill that she knew he was taking his last breaths and how it had been peaceful for him at the end, almost surreal. All the time I wanted to say something that made all this better for her, that could somehow take it away. I wanted to give her my imaginary friend so she could fly away to some better fan-tasy place and run through the fields like I'd done so many times when I'd felt sad but I didn't have the words inside. I couldn't do anything to make this better and that was something I'd always been good at, when someone cried I made them laugh, when someone was hurt I cleaned them, if some-thing was broken I fixed it and I felt so helpless that I couldn't do a thing to make this better. Mum still had her coat on. It was a black quilted coat and as I hugged her tightly I could smell her familiar Musk perfume, her scent tainted with the sadness of her tears tonight. I felt like I had done when she cried when Dad had worked away on the Island before we moved, so un-able to make her happy at that precise second.

As I lay in bed that night I searched my soul for some part to be sad for the loss of a family member that so many people loved, but there was no part of my soul left to mourn for him. I think he'd killed it. I examined over and over in my head whether I was to blame, whether God had had something to do with this. My relationship with God was beginning to fal-ter again after a brief resurrection because I didn't feel he would have done this to Mum, she didn't deserve it. Nana and Jill being there hadn't even come into my thoughts, all I could think of was my Mum for that night and what she was going through.

Early the next week when all the funeral arrangements had been set for the Friday and Grace and I had our permissions granted from school, Mum took Nana and Jill to the Chapel of Rest to say their last goodbyes. Dad drove them there in 'Grace's Golden Car', the Gold Sierra he had at the time because Mum couldn't deal with driving. She'd broken down in tears a few times that week, unable to see through the thick warm liquid and Dad didn't think it was fair for her to have to drive. Jill was coming back with Mum for a while afterwards to give Nana some space to herself so I was to stay in the spare room that night even though Jill would be staying at Nana's again with Mum, we had to keep the room clean for her and besides her clothes were in my wardrobe and her skin had been in my bed and I didn't want to create more work by cleaning the sheets again. I'd always been quite fussy about sleeping in sheets anyone else had slept in outside my immediate family. I loved staying in Mum, Dad or Grace's beds because of the secure smell that would fill my nose whilst I slept as if their own little personal smell kept away any evil spirits that may come for me in the night. Grace was very particular about her room though, only those invited were permitted and little sisters were definitely not allowed.

Dad's car was called Grace's Golden Car because of the letters in the registration – GGC. Even in Dad's car I couldn't match Grace. I wasn't as pure as her, I didn't do as well at school, she didn't put Mum and Dad through half the things I had, she was so bloody perfect. I think I viewed her in the same way as Nana was looking back at him, I thought of all the good things she did, not remembering the times she and Dad had argued about her coming home late, or the time when she'd vomited out of her bedroom window onto the flat roof above the kitchen because she'd been so pissed after a night out in town. In my eyes she did no wrong, when actually what she did do was pave the way for my life to be easier and more free than she'd even had. I think the older sibling generally does.

Nana fell that night on the way out of the Chapel of Rest, she fell hard against 'Graces Golden Car', you know because she didn't have enough to deal with at the time! She bruised the entire left hand side of her face like you wouldn't believe, bloody swelling intermingling with her tears as she dealt with the loss of her one true love. Funny thing love, you turn a blind eye to the cruel things someone you love does to you and concentrate on their good points and the things you want to remember, kind of like how hard it is to see the bad points of a relationship when you bump into your ex walking down the street with the most beautiful girl you've ever seen on his arm and you cry yourself stupid once you're out of sight.

That week before the funeral seemed to fly by in a daze. There were things to be organized, caterers to arrange, and the cards had started to come, flooding in from all different parts of the world, everybody passing their wishes and saying the world had lost something special.

Sat in Nana's front room, all of us dressed in Black, I looked out of the window at the shadow of the tree. It was morning and the sun was at the front of the house, however, the tree cast its shadow over the whole of the house, keeping us in semi darkness and although the sun was fairly bright it was a cold winter morning. The cars pulled up outside, the first one carrying the coffin and the second for us to travel to the crematorium in. Nana was wearing one of the fur coats I used to dress up in as a child and large dark glasses, partly to hide her tears, partly to hide the large black welt across her face. They were massive glasses that made it impossible to see what was going on behind them.

We got into the funeral cars. The procession was facing the wrong way so the traffic on the street waited as we drove around the grass verge opposite to face the top of the road where I had felt so much pain in my life. I sat on the front row of seats in the dreary Limousine looking out of the window on the right hand side behind the driver. I was surrounded by my family's tears although my thoughts were completely different and I felt nothing. I looked out of the opposite window at the pub, in particular at the wall that ran around the exterior of the plot of land it was built on and thought of all the times I'd walked on that wall holding tight to Nana's hand on the way back from the shops, or his hand on the way back from the Legion if we didn't take the short cut. I swear he used to take us that way just so we could walk on the wall. Right now I wanted to walk there. I wanted to be anywhere but in this car surrounded by the pain of everyone I loved. The car turned left at the top of the street past the grey entrance for Civic Centre, past the back of the Post Office were the cool kids hung out, looking for any little old person drawing pension so they could mug them. It seemed greyer today and the shadows of the high rise flats beyond reached to the road and filled the car with more gloom. And still I felt nothing.

We drove on past graffitied walls, grey flats, the tall railings at the side of the road and the kids fighting beyond them, until we turned into the road the Legion was on. The flag hanging from the front of the building was at half mast and the pavement was full of gentlemen in their uniforms, medals glistening in the cold sun. Someone was playing a trumpet, a slow mournful tune and these men, the same men who once told me stories so animatedly looked full of sorrow, some crying silently as they saluted one of their own off, maybe later than others that they'd cared about, but he was one of them nonetheless. Nana cried louder and louder until all I could feel in the car was a well of her pain. Mum was fairly quiet next to her but I knew she was crying silently.

I watched each face go by on the slow drive down towards the express-way that would lead us to his eventual resting place. Some men looked on respectfully, one guy in particular was wearing a white vest which struck me as odd as it was February and a bloody cold February at that. His tattoos covered his arms from top to bottom, like a second skin painted over the top. He looked fearsome, until he brought his hands to his face and made the sign of the cross and lowered his face in a mark of respect as we passed. In each face I searched for my imaginary friend, but he was nowhere to be seen today. Perhaps another of his girls needed him today, someone younger, someone helpless, not someone numb like me. The older gentle-men we now passed may have been without medals, but they all removed their flat caps as we passed, or signed themselves with the cross of Jesus. Even the kids that didn't normally stop for anything, were smacked round the head by their mothers and told to stand still, whilst the funeral of some poor lost soul went past on its melancholy journey.

As we turned into the Crematorium car park and the car pulled to a stop the familiar faces of people I knew and some I didn't looked expectantly at us through the windows. As we climbed out I saw Mike in his grey suit, the same suit he'd worn with a brightly coloured tie to their Golden Wedding, only this time his tie was black and I could see he had been crying. His moustache had got bushier over the years, but nothing else had changed about him at all, not a wrinkle, not a hair, nothing. His smile wasn't there today and I wanted to hug him and for him to throw me onto his shoulders and make me scream with laughter. Although I'd have probably broken his neck because I was about two feet taller than when he'd last done it! Then there were the strangers, the faces I didn't know, the people whose lives he'd touched that I had no knowledge of and by God there were hundreds of them. As the coffin was moved into the Crematorium and we his family moved into our places at the front, all the other people jostled to get a view of the service, a bit like they would queue at the market to get the best cuts of meat from the wrinkly butcher, each mourning their own individual loss. These people had been so kind to Nana over the last few months as she had dealt with his being at first in the hospital, then the hospice and now as she had prepared for and coped with the death of her husband. Death has that effect on people, doesn't it? It makes you forget being selfish for a moment and think about someone else and how they may cope.

As the vicar spoke about the goodness inside of him, his kindness in the charity work he did and the joy he gave his family I wanted to be sick. They stated he was a loving Grandfather to George, Sally, Wayne, Grace and Rachel, bullshit I was screaming in my head. Bullshit! (And in a house of God too!) Well screw God! He didn't help me when I needed him. He'd never come to me when I cried for help. So how could he be there to be an all seeing all hearing source of inspiration and light? How could he have let these things happen to me? Most of all how could he create something so monstrous on the one side and yet so loving and giving on the other that could inspire so many people to fill this large room with their grief? It just didn't make sense. That day was the end for me and God. The last straw. The final fling. It!

The congregation stood to sing 'Abide With Me' and Dad, whose hand had been getting warmer and warmer in mine as he stood next to me, slumped down further into the pew. His shoulders were shaking in grief, Gramps had always been there for him, they'd joked about football, Dad being a Manc and Gramps being a Blue, they'd always tormented each other, most of all Gramps had been there for Dad since his own Father had died, and for Dad he seemed to be losing his Father all over again. I studied the tears on my Dad's face as I stood to sing the hymn and laid the tissue in my hand gently into his then moved my hand to his shoulder. Dad had never cried in front of me before and it was so sad to see his eyes fill with water to the point where I didn't think they could hold anymore, and then suddenly burst letting two simultaneous tears run in perfect straight lines down his grief ridden face and drop onto his suit jacket creating a little circle of sadness that was visible for the next few hours. How could I ever say anything? How could I ever put Dad through this? I couldn't see Mum, she was too far in front of me and there were other people more important than Grace and I between us, however I could hear her, even over Nana's sobs my attuned ear could hear my own. How could I ever talk to anyone in this room when they all seemed so full of sorrow and love for this man?

As the first notes of John Lennon 'Imagine' filled the room and the curtains began to close I listened carefully to the words, my anger building and finally settling into tears of rage, which of course people mistook for sadness. He'd gone and died and left me to deal with everything now. He'd killed me inside, he'd taken everything and now the bastard was gone. My thoughts screamed 'BURN YOU BASTARD, BURN IN FUCKING HELL'! Outside I just felt into my small black bag for another tissue to wipe away this evidence of my emotion, like he'd wiped away the evidence on his dirty flannel.

As the song drew to a close and the curtains closed fully Nana was wailing so painfully that it stopped my head and we began to move outside and congregate on the grass verge. I searched all the faces for someone familiar as my family were all greeting guests, all tears gone now, eradicated by social duty calling. I found that friendly face in Shirley and Mark, two of Mum and Dad's best friends. I'd known them for what seemed like forever. Grace and I had grown up with their kids and they were exactly the familiar sight I needed right now. I hadn't seen them during the service, but Shirley's face was flushed with the tears she'd obviously cried inside the crematorium. It was strange really because in that moment I made a definition of friendship in my own head. They hadn't really been involved with Nana and Gramps, or not that I could recall anyway, yet here they were, just being there for us, our family, their friends. Shirley pulled me in, gave me a cuddle and told me she thought I'd been really brave. I didn't feel brave. I didn't feel anything about the funeral, however, I had a new found respect for them for coming, particularly for Mum, I knew it would mean a lot to her that they were there. I suppose a friend is someone who can feel your pain for you, who can cry for you, laugh with you and hold you when you need it and that's what Shirley was to Mum, a true friend.

We eventually got into the car again to make a faster journey this time back to the Legion. We were in the same faded room we'd been in many times before, the yellow wallpaper jaded with what seemed like a thousand years of cigarette smoke. Nana and Gramps had had their Golden Wedding Anniversary here, many of the same faces wandering around, only this time the buffet was better and the suits darker, devoid of colour.

Mike was sitting at the bar, the stool next to him empty, he stayed there for at least five minutes seemingly remembering, with his space next to him, who used to fill it, just sitting, before he became his usual self again walking from one table to the next cracking jokes and laughing his booming laugh, like the son that Gramps had never had. People that had cried not a hour before laughed and made jolly with friends they hadn't seen in a while and Mum drifted around from group to group, all the while keeping a watchful eye on Nana who sat at the 'top table' whilst people came to talk to her and hold her hand in condolence. Grace's eyes were raw from crying but when I went to the toilet and stared into the mirrors I hadn't been able to see into as a child, I looked no different. Yes sure my hair had grown and my face was wiser, not much, but a bit, but nothing seemed different. My eyes were normal.

Mike came over and put his arm around me and sat talking to me for a long time. It felt strange that someone I loved so much as a child should still see me as a child now. If only he knew how grown up I was inside, he wouldn't talk to me as he was then. Maybe he'd have felt differently about his loss if he'd have known. Maybe everybody would have done.

I couldn't eat any of the beautiful buffet. They had obviously made a real effort down at the Legion to give him a good old fashioned send off and it seemed strange to me that these people could be so shallow to mourn one minute and then bam, the tears were gone and they were acting as though nothing had happened, laughing, joking and filling their faces.

The vinyl floor was old and worn around the bar and the carpet under the table felt sticky against my shoes. I sat studying the bottles of alcohol and fizzy pop behind the bar from my seat. They still sold the same brand of cheap crisps and to the most part nothing did seem to have changed. I felt in a timewarp, looking around at all the familiar sights, the uniformed war veterans reminiscing about times gone by, memories as sad as mine.

In my head I played over these memories wishing I could be like Nana and only remember the good things, but try as I may I couldn't. I could think of his body going up into the smoke that I had seen curling out of the top of the Crematorium as we drove away. I could almost feel the heat that he would be feeling now, except he wouldn't feel it, his pain was all gone now. Not like the pain inside me. He would feel nothing, perhaps the same numbness I felt now. I tried to mourn for my Gramps, the distinction between Gramps and Granddad wickedly distorted in my memory. How could I even make that distinction now? In years to come how could I apply the same amount of clarity to my previous distinction? Would I be able to remember just the good times, the good times people were reminiscing over now, laughing at their own personal memory and take on a situation?

I thought about the visits I'd made to the hospice to see him, sitting there in his brown pyjamas, the same ones he'd worn when he had come to me. I thought about Aunty Julie and I standing outside, sneaking off for a fag when no one was watching. Julie was the cool aunty. Everyone has one! She was the one who swore, drank and smoked and always told you how it was in straight terms. She'd listened to me over the countless boy troubles and trivial things I had suffered in my life and I know if I'd have told her the things I was going through she would probably be the one person who wouldn't judge me or question me. She'd just have held me.

I thought about the first time I had realized in the hospice that I was now stronger and how that had made me feel. It had been my dream to be stronger physically than him. In my dreams I'd stuck up for myself with him, I'd said no and I'd told with no consequences because I was the stronger one.

All these thoughts whizzing around and around inside my head whilst I made nice with the people who seemed to care about him.

At that moment I caught sight of him, out of the window, my imaginary friend, just checking up on me. He must have had a break in his schedule of all the other girls he looked after, for he was there, smiling. He could see my thoughts and he knew that I was now safe. He wasn't needed anymore because no one could ever hurt me again. I was his safe and sound girl now and although in my dreams he had been the one to rescue me, in the end, I hadn't needed rescuing anymore. I had realized at some point along the way that I couldn't marry this man with no penis, as much as I loved him. I needed to marry a man who could be there for me all the time, who could love me warts and all, and maybe that would be Martin, maybe it wouldn't, I would just have to wait and see.

So the day I buried my Granddad, I also buried deep inside of me the most important friend of my life, the man at the window, my confidant, my first love, my best friend, my partner in crime, my imaginary friend, the man whom everyone from then on would be compared to and have to live up to in my mind.

That night as Martin and I walked up the bumpy road from the house in Lymm, to our local pub to meet up with our normal Friday night friends I took a deep breath in, inhaling the cold fresh smell of my freedom from him, my thoughts still swimming around my head, my screwed up emotions, but one sticking out with such clarity and venom that it shocked me.

'Burn you bastard, burn! I hope you burn in hell for what you've done!'

Chapter 12

The Afterlife

All had changed now!

A few weeks prior to his death I had contacted Social Services to see about obtaining counseling for what had happened. I needed it now more than ever as he seemed to be waiting for me behind every door, only now he was so badly disfigured from the fire that his face had become distorted to me. My message had been passed through to Kirsten's Mum who was the on duty Social Worker that day and she obviously couldn't have handled my situation being an acquaintance of sorts, however, within the next few weeks I was contacted by a lady named Kath who made an appointment for me to come and talk to her at Hilden House in town. Martin picked me up in his Dad's car and drove me to town that day. He parked outside on the double yellow lines, only for a second, so as he could kiss me and watch me walk through the door, believing his work had been done until afterwards when he would pick up the 'pieces of Rach' from the floor.

I sat in the office at first waiting to meet her, petrified of what I was doing, most of all scared that Mum and Dad would become involved. However, my overriding fear was that there would come a day, maybe even some day soon that the pain would become too unbearable and I would do something that I would regret, I would take my self-harm too far and damage myself as much physically as I was emotionally.

The minute Kath walked across the room I could see her gentleness radiating out. She had very kind eyes and didn't mind that I didn't want to shake hands, she just accepted it. She led me into a dreary and dark room, the only window being a long, thin line up high and the glass was frosted so that people could neither see in or out. It didn't feel like a safe room. I wanted Martin to be there but he was somewhere outside with his own thoughts. I knew that she was there for me, however I'd made the decision that I couldn't tell her anything in this room. It wasn't right for me there and then. I'd made a huge mistake. So I did what I normally did and talked about the other things around the larger issue. I diverted every question about my Granddad apart from to tell her he was dead and that I wished that I could in some way tell my parents without them judging me. She tried her hardest to reassure me that this wouldn't happened, although I was so non-committal she must have felt so frustrated, if for nothing more than she could see this girl in front of her that so desperately wanted some-one to talk to but would not open up.

When she called me to arrange the second appointment I didn't go. I couldn't bear the thought of sitting in that grey room again. That was the last contact I had with Social Services.

Martin was finding it increasingly difficult to understand why I did the things I did. He couldn't grasp why I would put myself through the ordeal of going to Nana's house and staying over, when I came home so screwed up at the end of the weekend having been taunted by the ghosts of my past. I had been adept at containing my feelings to the extent that he didn't know that I saw Granddad wherever I went, in my head, anyway, that I didn't have to be there at 172 for the memories to be flowing through my veins. I think that this was when he first started seeing people behind my back and I suppose in a way I was partly to blame because I'd pushed him away to the extent that he felt unable to help me anymore. Our relation-ship would drift in and out of this pattern for the next two and a bit years until we finally went our own separate ways, granted both hurt deeply, although we knew it was for the best.

Either Martin drove me to Nana's if Mum wasn't available to take me over or I would get the bus, which I hated. The kids that hung out on the corner no longer seemed cool, more menacing for a middle class girl like myself. One time I arrived so late, as Mum and Dad were away on holiday and the bus had been stuck in traffic between Altrincham and Wythen-shawe, that it was almost pitch black as we pulled into the bus station on the other side of the market. This would mean walking through Muggers Alley and Civic by myself with a bag of clothes, putting myself in what I perceived to be so much danger. As I climbed off the bus the station was deserted, except of course that is, for Granddad, who read the paper on one of the benches, peered around the corner of the high building at the far side, who watched from the other side of the Perspex that was full of graffiti and who followed as my pace quickened to get through this journey as swiftly as I could. As I turned into Muggers Alley I could hardly see anything in the dark. So much so that I rushed straight into a dark figure walking slowly and silently through. My whole body tensed as adrenalin surged through my arms, until that is I heard the crackle of his radio, and looked to see the Community Bobby on his nightly patrol. I was so relived to see him. It was something that was a rarity then, even more so now, to have a Bobby on the beat and as I apologized for rushing into him I explained that the bus had been delayed and I wanted to get to Nana's house as quick as I could. He turned around to face the opposite entrance to the Alley and began to walk silently with me through Civic centre, past the pub where I longed to walk on the wall holding this stranger's hand and down to 172. I don't know if it was out of kindness or whether he thought I was up to no good, but he walked me the full distance, seeming relieved when Nana recognized my voice and opened the door to let me in. I thanked him again and again and Nana offered him a cup of tea, but he simply said that we were both welcome and he must get on. I'm sure he had more important things to do than to see a frightened girl home, however he hadn't made me feel like that. He waited outside until he heard us lock the door and then went on his way. For the first time in my life I hadn't been afraid of a Policeman. I was so proud of myself. I felt like his brainwashing was wearing off finally. I'd managed to put enough distance between myself and the abuse that it seemed almost surreal. But for the fact I still saw him I might have been able to pack it away in a box in my head and never go there again.

Inside the house his pictures were everywhere, adorning each room and wall with his friendly smile, always a glass in his hand. He no longer seemed burnt in my mind or when I saw him, the pictures changing his form for me, as it always changed here, back to being his normal face, not the translucent face he had developed in Cancer, but the scary face he had when he became Granddad.

The house felt somewhat empty now and it seemed to me Nana was starting to let herself go slightly. Since Whisky had died she had got another cat called Rupert. Rupert was a huge monster of a cat, fat, contented and a bit more fat. He curled up each night at Nana's feet in front of the fire, or almost full length of the sofa if he stretched as he often did in his full state.

It felt strange to be watching the television, particularly shows with cheesy jingles in, the ones he had muted the television for and as they blurted out their cheery music it was like a reminder that he was dead and gone. The adverts blared into the room as they never had before in between the programmes and Nana seemed to keep the sound for company. Her spoons now lay dusty on the racks as Grace and I no longer polished them to please her when we came round. The mats in the Kitchen stuck to the table with dust and the house constantly smelt of the fish that she cooked for the cat. The Bear on the fireplace was also surrounded by a thick layer of dust, only unsettled when I occasionally held him in my hand to feel something familiar. Whether she didn't see the dust, as her eye sight was deteriorating, or whether she just gave up now she no longer had the will nor the inclination to clean her house just for herself, I don't know. I always helped her clean a little whilst I was there, as if cleaning the house would somehow cleanse my memories, except of course it didn't matter how hard I cleaned, the house would always mean something different to me than anyone else. Somehow dirtier than Nana could ever let it get.

The back scratcher stood to attention in its stand, as though it were waiting for its master to return so scratch some poor little innocent girl's back. I would sometimes sit and touch the plastic prongs trying to make sense of this memory or that. In fact it was like the whole house missed him like Nana did, like my family did, and in some ways like I missed my Gramps. I think that's what Martin found the hardest to understand and I suppose sometimes I did too. How I could miss someone who had scarred me so deeply and in the worst way imaginable. In my mind, despite my fears at his funeral, I always had the distinction between Granddad and my Gramps.

The picture I had drawn for him all those years ago of him in flares with the brandy glass in his hand still hung on the cupboard in the kitchen. The 'What is a Grandfather' Plaque still hung above the cooker next to the window I had wished myself out off so many times I'd lost count. What is a Grandfather? Because I sure as hell had a twisted view of him. I wanted so much to have what the poem said, the love, the warmth and the special bond that it spoke of. We'd had a 'special' bond, a destructive, dark special bond. Who was I special to now?

The table in the Kitchen was now covered in cat hairs, as was the once shiny sugar bowl, with its coal shovel spoon. The sugar was grey.

Nana no longer bought me Garlic Sausage and Cottage Cheese when I came over and although I didn't ever see her cry I knew she missed him desperately as it took several sleeping tablets to get her off to sleep at night. I used to pray that I would get to sleep before her when I stayed because if I didn't I would be kept awake all night by her loud snore and that is when my ghosts would surface more frequently. His silent creep across the floor, his giggle, the clink of his glass as he poured himself a drink and his drunken ramblings filled the house in every which direction I listened.

We always walked to the Market when I went over, people stopping to talk to Nana and asking her in a sympathetic voice, with their heads tipped to one side, how she was feeling. I found it condescending to listen to their false wishes, because I felt if she actually started to tell them how she felt without the one true love of her life, that they wouldn't listen, although perhaps that is unfair of me. Perhaps they really did care.

Even the insides of Nana's jewelry box had developed its own form of chaos. No longer were earrings lined up and necklaces laid side by side, they were strewn in a random fashion as if she too had had a dressing up session to feel like a film star in front of the mirror and then just thrown them back when she tired of her childish games.

I always took my school work with me and this particular night I was revising for my upcoming exams. The pressure of all this pent up anger inside me was taking its toll on my life and I was spending a lot of time either wagging school or not going in through illness.

This particular night I felt tormented to the point of distraction. I wanted so well to make Mum and Dad proud of me in these exams, but one of my teachers had told me I would fail so what was the use.

As I lay awake listening to my memories in a noisy silence, I could hear the creaking of the tree at the front, gently rocking in the wind. I could hear the wind whistling its way through the leaves and imagined that they would float off over Civic and the park as I had once flown away with my imaginary friend to escape my place of torture and above these noises my thoughts shouted at me. I knew I needed to try to get help again before this situation took me lower than I would be able to recover from.

When I returned home that weekend and sat at the relative safety of my window ledge surrounded by more familiar noises and smells, I made the decision to go to my Doctor. My family Doctor was a wonderful man. He'd seen me since I was ten and he liked our family, I knew that as he told Mum and Dad every time they went what nice girls they had, because we always had a smile, even when the earth felt like it was crashing around me I had my painted smile for him. He had kind eyes and he was a Christian man who seemed so fair and gentle.

As I sat in front of him years of pent up frustration came out in the form of tears. Tears that streamed and splattered down my cheeks with such ferocity that it shocked me. I told him about being touched, in a dirty way, I told him how it made me feel now Granddad was dead and he said nothing. Just watched me with his gentle eyes. There were brightly coloured tissues on his desk but he never offered me one, my tears would have dried up if he had, I'd have felt like he wanted my tears to dry up and go away, so I'm glad he didn't because right then I needed to cry. When I had finished he sat back in his chair and began to explain to me that I had a journey of healing to start. He wanted clarity that I was no longer in any danger first and foremost and then he set about giving me some ideas for solutions, the first being more Counseling at the surgery, the second being anti-depressants to help me cope.

I accepted both because I trusted him. He was the first man, outside of my family, that I did completely trust. He was such a support to me that day and I finally felt my secret was being shared in a productive way for me. I still hadn't had the courage to share that I saw Granddad frequently, or that I looked to inflict pain on myself, but I'd made a start and that was one of the hardest things to do.

The first appointment I had for my Counseling was so completely different to my last experience. The counselor, Caz, was no different to Kath (equally as kind), however the room was bright and airy and the window looked inviting. For my first session I felt I was at the window, inhaling the fresh air from outside as Martin talked to Caz for me, trying to explain in his words what he felt I was going through.

At the end of the session she explained that, although it was wonderful that I had such support from my boyfriend, she felt that it would be more beneficial to just be the two of us next time. I agreed to an appointment the following week and although I felt uncomfortable in the waiting room next time round, I had begun to accept that she was right. I could get Martin to talk for me as much as I wanted, however in doing that I was avoiding dealing with the issue myself. For the whole of the second hour that I spent with Caz I cried, not saying anything, just crying and she let me! It felt like the longest hour and I'm sure it must have been longer for her, but in that hour I began to let down my barriers, for the next time, when my story began with her. Funny thing is she never gave me any advice, she simply acted as a mirror and helped me come to my own conclusions.

I talked to her about everything. My relationship with him, how it had turned me to use sex as a weapon for affection and acceptance and we, together, worked through my issues one by one as they arose.

It must have been working because one night after a particularly tiring session I sat on a ledge at the top of Slitten Brook looking down the sheer drop and thinking. For the first time as I thought about my life, I didn't want to jump, I didn't want to hurt myself and I most certainly didn't want to be someone else. One of the lads from my year at school, Damien, that I'd had a crush on for the first three years of High School had walked past, seen me and climbed down to sit with me. Whereas before I would have used this opportunity to have sex with him, we sat and talked. I told him everything and he held me. No sex, no kissing, he just held me as I sobbed. I think that was the first moment I realized I would eventually be healed of my darkness. It was also my first step towards acceptance by the other kids at school. It was just a shame that I was coming to the end of my school life when I was finally starting to fit in.

So my life had changed, all had changed, everything that I'd known for so long, but more importantly my sightings of him started to decrease as I became stronger. I could fight now, I was in the position of strength.

I sat my GCSE's not expecting much, however to my delight I did quite well, got good enough grades to prove my English Teacher wrong, who had constantly graded me at a C/D over the last two years. The external markings had given me two B's for my English and I was delighted. In my final act of defiance at school I walked past her waving my results in the air in a victory, for in my life she was insignificant, unimportant, I had the world at my feet and I was going to set it alight with the new attitude that I was working on in my Counseling.

Mum and Dad were proud of me for my results, if not some what shocked because I'd never seemed to revise properly to them. Most of all I was proud of myself, ok it didn't last long, but for a few days I was proud of what I had achieved, for I felt that being 'special' had made me destined to be a failure for the rest of my life, however now I had proved that I had a head on my shoulders and not just a brain full of daydreams whether they be good or bad. My life was on the up now and I was so determined that it was going to continue doing so, I didn't know how, but I didn't really care. I was healing and it felt good.

Chapter 13

The End

I have spent the majority of my adult life, so far, living in a child's world, a result of being forced to grow up so young.

In many ways I feel like the butterfly I held all those years ago, as though Granddad touched my wings and made me unable to fly anymore, perhaps even killed my soul. I told a friend of mine Emmanouil the story of the butterfly. He told me his mother used to say if a butterfly lost its dust to put it into the flowers. He said he'd never yet found a dead butterfly there. So maybe that's where I am now. Maybe I'm in flowers and my dust is being restored. If I'll ever fly again I don't know, but recovery feels good. Perhaps this, my moment in the 'flowers' will be my 'jellonet square', still leaving me with emotional scars however, eventually, it may be my healing.

I still don't like my birthday, even now some twenty three years later I cannot deal with the day, which is daft really because it's just another day. My flashbacks seem to get much worse around that time of year.

I know now, from speaking to other survivors of his hand, that I actually was 'special' to him and the relationship we shared differed greatly to his abuse to the others. There were few he penetrated and he seemed to have (I loathe to say this but it best describes how I feel) behaved with more leniency to others. Not that any kind of abuse can be considered worse, better, stronger, weaker or more lenient, be it physical, emotional or sexual abuse, it is my opinion that as much damage can be done by any of the three.

Moving to the now, even when we have our differences my family are still there for me. They are a source of inspiration, support and love everyday, even when I have treated them badly through the darker times in my life, they have always been there. Family to me is something which you do not need to worry about losing, even in death, although as much as I feel loathing for myself for saying it, there is one half of a member of my family I am grateful for losing. I feel a family may not have to speak every five minutes to know they are there for each other, they just are. I know I can call on any member of my family and they will be there for me and it's a given that I will be there for them. However, I have yet to find a grown up, be it in or outside my family, who understands me completely. Many have tried and failed. Maybe it is because in all truth I don't understand myself most of the time. The way I react to things, the way I find myself behaving on occasion and the way I am never going to become a fully fledged, paid up member of this society we call 'being a grown up'. I still struggle with the fact that I am now 29 years old and have responsibilities that I need to behave like an adult for, for part of me is still locked in a childhood that pushed me to grown up quicker yet made me the eternal child.

Sometimes I feel used, sometimes scared, sometimes angry at him, sometimes I love him, one thing I don't have and will never have is understanding for what he did to me. It has become apparent that he did this to other members of my family, their names are not for me to mention and their stories are different to mine. We have since found out he touched other people's children but that the parents of the two girls that we know about didn't prosecute because of my Nana, 'that nice Mrs Mainwaring lady'. That lady didn't owe anybody in my family any loyalty but she chose to give it.

I think one of the hardest decisions I have faced whilst writing down my experiences is the fact that some of my family disagree with the fact I am recording my life in this way, but do you know what, it has helped. It was hard but it has helped. I know that some of them won't be able to read it and I respect that. It is their choice. I have loyalty to my family, the family that love and care for me, however I refuse to keep my secret anymore because I am not naughty! I am not a bad girl! I am brave and courageous and that is something that he, nor anybody else, can ever take away from me.

Of all the people who I could have told in my family, of all the people who could have helped me, I didn't and for that I still feel in some way that I let them down when really the only person I let down is myself. I could have told earlier. I could have said something but I chose not to. For whatever reason, it was my decision. It has made me determined to try to lead some kind of normal existence but there are obviously ways in which my experiences affect my life now. They have moulded me into a different person, given me a fierce determination to succeed, a strong love of those around me, an inability to say no, an inability to deal with confrontation and an intense and passionate protective instinct for my family and close friends.

I have instilled in my daughter, from birth, the ability to be able to tell me anything no matter what it is and no matter what anybody says will happen. However, would she have the words to be able to vocalise something so incomprehensible at her age? Probably not. I know I didn't.

My parents have questioned themselves over and over again if there was anything that they could have done. And the answer is quite simply no! There is one person and one person alone to blame.

My Granddad.

Not Gramps, the friendly guy from the Legion, but Granddad that appeared at the bottom of a bottle every day. I have asked myself so many times if he drank to get away from his disappointment in himself, or disgust, or self-hatred. However, I think I may be trying too hard to apply logic to it, a logic that doesn't really exist in this situation.

What makes somebody do that? What makes a grown man physically, emotionally destroy a five year old child's body and spirit. Nobody knows, because if 'they' did 'they' would invent something, some kind of drug that could eradicate thoughts from the mind of a pedophile.

As for my imaginary friend, going back to find him whilst writing this book was an incredibly hard thing to do. Yet his face was the same as I remembered. He still had gentle, liquid eyes and he still reminded me of Dad. I am a dreamer and I think I always will be. I think the difference now is that I understand the distinction between reality and my window adventures. I can still have my dream world now and again, I can still live at the window. The pleasure now being I have a choice as to whether I go there. My reality is better than my dream world and that is really the whole point to my story, apart from being very cathartic for me to write. I am living proof you can move on from something so horrific, so dreadful that you feel your life is over and that you can't go on. I am a walking survivor, more than that I will not just survive, I will thrive!

It has been my life long ambition to work in the caring profession, a dream which I am rapidly closing in on. I am applying for the qualifications I need to achieve. I am taking back some pride in myself and the work I can do. Writing the words has been therapeutic but also necessary for me to move on with my life and put this into a box in my head where I'll only go if I need to. If I can take these experiences I've had and change them into something positive by working in the community, well I've succeeded! I know it will be tough, but I can do it.

I've reached a crossroads in my life where I no longer have to be afraid. I don't have to use an imaginary friend for comfort and support because I have myself, and do you know what, I'm actually ok. I can write about the good times and the bad experiences and I can cry over them both and that's healthy for me. That's the way it should be.

When I was a child, an innocent, screwed up, helpless, lonely, desolate, depressed child, I would always start a story with once upon a time and finish it with the end. For me writing this story has been exactly that - the end.

About the Author

After a flirtation with recruitment, Rachel spent a few years working as a Personal Assistant within Advertising and subsequently the IT sector. After the death of her son and the following year's birth of her daughter, Rachel worked for a professional sports psychologist within the English Football Premier League, eventually moving onto Sales and subsequently becoming an at home mum.

Having lived through abuse from an Alcoholic, Rachel is currently studying Alcohol and Drugs Counseling as a stepping-stone towards her goal of becoming a Social Worker, whilst working part time and writing her second book. She is also currently developing her website (www.rachel-farrington-allen.co.uk) where she is setting up a forum designed for survivors of abuse to share their thoughts, feelings and stories. She has participated in several workshops and courses in sexual abuse and counseling and hopes to work in this area with children who have suffered as a result of another's actions.

She has done voluntary work within schools, using creativity to help children learn, Nursing homes, and spent a few years as a Childminder.

Her greatest achievement, besides her writing, was leading Australia out at the 2002 Commonwealth Games as a volunteer representing Manchester.

When not working or writing, Rachel spends most of her time at home with her daughter, Lucie to whom she is devoted and plays an active role in her school and schooling. She lives in Cheshire.

ISBN 1-41205514-8

9 781412 055147